One Foot in Front of the Other

-

First Steps

by

Neil Rawlins

Text & Photography
©2018 Neil S. Rawlins

All Rights Reserved

*"Travel, after all, requires no special experience –
All one has to do is place one foot in front of the other"*
Sanche de Gramont
The Strong Brown God

Table of Contents

Introduction		1
Chapter 1	Little Barrier	7
Chapter 2	The *Tofua* Voyage	15
Chapter 3	Return to Little Barrier	27
Chapter 4	Auckland to Kathmandu	39
Chapter 5	India	52
Chapter 6	Pakistan, Afghanistan & Iran	69
Chapter 7	Turkey to London	88
Chapter 8	Travels in Britain & France	108
Chapter 9	Journey to the U.S.S.R.	125
Chapter 10	U.K. Days	148
Chapter 11	Across the Sahara to Kano	173
Chapter 12	Central Africa to Nairobi	188
Chapter 13	Hitching to Johannesburg	207
Chapter 14	Return to New Zealand	220
Postscript		238

Introduction

I had always wanted to travel. When I was growing up in New Zealand, the comings and goings of ships at the port of Auckland always fascinated me. They were undoubtedly going to exotic places and who knew when they would be back again. My father worked as a customs-clearing agent for John Burns, an Auckland importer, and had to spend much of his time down at the docks. On a regular basis, when he arrived home after a hard day's work, I would ask: "What ships are in port today?" or "Is the *Cumberland* in yet?" I'm not quite sure why the *Cumberland* was such a favourite; I must have seen it docked at some stage. New Zealand was still very remote from the rest of the World – literally the ends of the earth. Air transport was slowly gaining the ascendancy with PanAm flying the four-engine triple-tailed Lockheed Super Constellation aircraft from North America. TEAL, which became Air New Zealand, flew Solent flying boats to Australia and on the Coral route to Fiji, Cook Islands and Tahiti. In the early 1960s BOAC, which later became British Airways, flew de Havilland Comets, the first jet aircraft, into Whenuapai which was then the International Airport. Our home in the Auckland north-western suburb of Te Atatu was on the flight path to Whenuapai.

When I was about 12 my maternal grandfather's younger brother paid the extended family a visit from

Western Samoa where he lived, and we all went down to see him off home. It was an emotional experience. We watched the Union Shipping Company's *Matua* back slowly away from the wharf. A band was playing *Now is the Hour*, and thousands of paper streamers stretched, broke and fluttered away in the evening breeze. My cousins were crying their eyes out with the tears of a last farewell as they knew they would not see their grandfather again. It is one of those lingering childhood memories that is etched on my mind.

There were also other connections with the great wide world away from New Zealand's fair shores. A friend of my parents, who had prematurely lost her husband, travelled to Europe to attend the Olympic Games in Rome in 1960. For a time, I periodically received postcards from her, and when I last heard from her, she was living in Majorca. As far as I know, she never returned to New Zealand. Also, my primary school teacher, a Scotsman named George Bell, had travelled widely and we pupils would often try to side-track him from teaching us boring things like arithmetic or grammar into telling us stories of his experiences. Although he knew what we were up to, he would usually good-humouredly oblige with some little anecdote from Africa, or Asia, or Scotland! One holiday he sent me a postcard from New Caledonia – in it he told me it was the fiftieth country he had visited. I was impressed. So I guess it was logical that in my adult years I would travel and eventually end up with a career in the travel industry.

During the 1960s the Overland route through Asia had become popular with young people, especially during the hippy era in the later years of that decade and Kathmandu was the ultimate goal. I was by then working as a clerical officer with the Department of Lands & Survey in Auckland and my mind became focused on eventually heading offshore. Asia appealed, although I would never have called myself a hippy in those days. In the late '60s my travels began, first to the Pacific Islands on the 'banana' boat *Tofua* and a year or so later on a short trip to Fiji with my mother. During the course of my duties with the Lands & Survey Department, I was fortunate enough to visit two of the remoter bird sanctuary islands of Auckland's Hauraki Gulf which the Department then administered. This gave me a taste of adventures closer to home.

It was in 1970 that I eventually set off, travelling on an organised overland tour through Asia. I had my SLR camera, bought in Fiji, in hand with instructions to take lots of photos, which I did, and all sorts of other helpful advice such as "Don't talk to strange men!" from an aunt who meant well but …! I did not, of course, then know how influential this first Overland trip would be for me. Nine years later I was back, this time as a tour leader, but those experiences will be recounted in another book.

I enjoyed the Overland through Asia very much, it was definitely an eye-opener. This was my kind of travel. I was lucky enough to travel through Afghanistan in happier, calmer days when it was a kingdom and through an Iran still at peace with the world, although there was a simmering undercurrent of internal tensions against the Shah. After working in England for a year, I took a tour to the Soviet Union, then a mysterious and somewhat scary place if one was to believe Western propaganda, this being the height of the Cold War with Leonid Brezhnev and his grey-suited apparatchiks being in firm control. St Petersburg was still called Leningrad, we were one of the first Western tour groups to visit Kharkov, not long recovered from the devastations of World War Two, and not too many groups had visited Kiev and Odessa in the Ukraine.

In the UK I was primarily employed as a farm worker – the general consensus in those days being that if you were a New Zealander you must be a farmer. It was work I enjoyed and although it was one of the lowest paid jobs in the UK, I could save more than I could in higher paid work in London. I saved on accommodation costs and, at times of the year, there was quite a lot of overtime. I eventually saved enough to return to New Zealand by the Overland route through Africa.

The African Overland was something quite different and in the '70s was nowhere near as politically hazardous as it is today. Colonialism had only recently ended, and the newly independent nations were still finding their feet. Most of the problems at this time, were those created by the eccentricities of local dictators such as Idi Amin in Uganda, Mobutu Sese Seko in the Congo and Jean-Bedel Bokassa in the Central African Republic. UN sanctions were in place against Rhodesia, then under the UDI of Ian Smith, and there was a bloody guerrilla war being fought against the Portuguese overlords in Mozambique.

The highlight of my African expedition was the crossing of the Sahara and this again was to stand me in good stead years later when I began operating Camel Safaris in Rajasthan for Explore Worldwide. There is something about deserts that attracts me. The African Overland tour ended in Nairobi and I hitch-hiked most of the way through southern Africa, working for a time in Johannesburg before finally catching a ship from Cape Town back to New Zealand.

This book is a narrative of these first travels compiled from diaries, letters home, articles, photographs and memories. The world was still a place of innocence although, saying that, terrorism was just beginning to rear its ugly head, but it was still a long way from the toxic, indiscriminate form it now takes. In those days travellers were, more or less, sacrosanct. Borders, although slow, were never really a problem as long as you stuck to the rules, were patient, humoured the border officials and didn't try to smuggle drugs or firearms. Most of the delays were of an arrogant bureaucratic nature but then you just accepted that. If you got angry, or impatient, you could be waiting twice as long. There was no social media in those days and the only contact with home would be a rather infrequent letter or postcard which hopefully wouldn't be misplaced, or an even more infrequent, expensive telephone call. In cases of emergency there was the telegramme, or if you could find one, a telex.

The fond memories of this era are always with me and can never be taken away. To quote the written words of George Westbrook, my maternal great grandfather: *"I have achieved nether riches nor possessions; but I have long, gallant memories of the Vanished Years that no man can wrest from me ..."*

Eheu, fugaces labuntur anni - alas, the fleeting years go by (Horace 65Bc – 8BC)

All thanks to Jan, my long suffering, supportive wife, who does not appear on the scene until the next book.

Chapter 1   Little Barrier

Ever since I was at school I knew I would travel. I had grown up in New Zealand in the fifties and sixties and the world had always seemed so very far away. By the end of the sixties air travel was beginning to become affordable and the world was slowly becoming more accessible. However, there was still a mystique about the outside world and my imagination would run wild with dreamy images of painted domes, perfumed gardens, palaces with inlaid balconies and exquisite temples to mysterious pagan gods. It was an age for a young romantic. In my teenage years I had been inspired by Peter Pinney's book, *Dust on My Shoes*. This was about an overland journey he had made through Asia just after World War Two. Peter Pinney had hitch-hiked and travelled by local transport from civil-war racked Greece to the dangerous steaming jungles of Burma where his Dutch travelling companion had drowned in the monsoon-swollen Chindwin River. Despite its tragic ending, the book had given me an intrinsic interest in the Overland route to Europe from India. Little did I know just how familiar this route would become in later decades.

During my formative years my family did not travel much. We visited relations in Palmerston North and in Northland, and in my later teenage years went on fun skiing trips to Tongariro National Park. Much of our holiday time had been spent developing our family bach (holiday home) at Army Bay on the Whangaparaoa

Peninsula just north of Auckland city. Dad had been born in England and his family had emigrated to New Zealand just after the First World War. He was just 6 years old when they arrived in Auckland. The only other time he had left New Zealand's shores was during World War 2 when, with the 3rd New Zealand Division, he had seen active service in Fiji, New Caledonia, New Hebrides and the Solomon Islands.

My mother's ancestry was far more colourful. Her maternal great-grandparents were John Milsome Jury, an English sailor, and Te Aitu-o-te-Rangi, daughter of the Maori chief Te Whatahoronui of the Wairarapa. According to family tradition John Milsome Jury had jumped ship in the Bay of Islands from a British whaler and had ended up on Kapiti Island, near Wellington, the stronghold of the Maori war chief Te Rauparaha. Here he met Te Aitu, whose father had been killed by a Te Ati Awa war party in the late 1830s, and she had been taken into captivity. Much to Te Rauparaha's displeasure the couple fell in love and fled from Kapiti Island to the Wairarapa where they evaded their pursuers, were married by William Williams, an early missionary in New Zealand, and eventually developed a farm near the modern town of Carterton.

My maternal grandmother, Ruby May Jury – John and Te Aitu's grand-daughter, had been regarded as the 'belle of the Wairarapa' in the early 20th century and was sent first to stay with relatives in Ballarat in Australia and then to her father's plantations in Tonga and Samoa to escape the attentions of a suitor of whom the family did not approve. In Samoa she met, fell in love and eventually married my grandfather, John Westbrook, whose English father, George, was a well-known trader in Apia. George Westbrook, once described by the American author Julian Dana as 'Samoa's Greatest Adventurer', had had a checkered and colourful career first as a supercargo on a number of small trading schooners and later as a trader in a several smaller Pacific islands including Pingalap in Micronesia, Funafuti in modern Tuvalu, Rotuma in Fiji and Wallis Island, now a French territory, where my grandfather was born. After losing almost everything on Wallis Island in the violent hurricane of 1889 (the same hurricane that famously destroyed 3 American and 3 German warships in Apia Harbour) George Westbrook set himself up as a trader in Apia, where he remained for the rest of his life. My grandfather and grandmother returned to New Zealand with their young family at the end World War 1, where my mother, the fourth sibling in a family of six, was born. Mum's oldest brother, affectionately known to the family as 'Winks', was killed on 1st December 1941 in the Battle of Sidi Rezegh during the attempted relief of Tobruk.

I grew up in Te Atatu, a suburb of Auckland, where Dad had had a house built on a section of land he had bought in the early 1950s for £155 from Hec Ramsay, creator of the famous wooden 'buzzy bee' toy. Dad later told me that Hec Ramsay refunded him £20 as he felt he had overcharged! When we moved to Te Atatu Auckland's North-Western motorway had not been constructed, although the first two-laned section was completed shortly afterwards. All my primary schooling was at the old Te Atatu Primary and my secondary education at the newly opened Rutherford High School. In 1960 my parents had begun building a holiday home, the bach, at Army Bay on the Whangaparaoa Peninsula north of Auckland in which my sister Valerie and I had many happy holidays with our friends during our formative teenage years.

I left school at the end of 1965 and began working, in January 1966, as an administration clerk at the Department of Lands & Survey, then situated in the old Customs House on the corner of Albert and Custom Streets in downtown Auckland. The work was varied and could be interesting. In those days the Lands & Survey in Auckland administered the islands of the Hauraki Gulf, including the bird sanctuary of Little Barrier Island with which I had an early fascination. Special permission had to be obtained to visit the Island, normally restricted to ornithologists, educationists and scientists. Its bluish, cloud-capped peaks could be seen on the misty horizon from our Army Bay bach.

In the last week of November 1966, I was called into the office of Darcy O'Brien, then assistant Commissioner of Crown Lands, and asked if I would like to go to Little Barrier for a week to help the resident ranger, Rodger Blanshard, build a new generator shed. Rodger's wife and family were away and there would be just the two of us on the island. I naturally jumped at this opportunity. The following Saturday morning I left

Westhaven on the HMNZS *Ngapona*, a motor defence launch operated by the Royal New Zealand Navy Reserve. The weather was a bit rough and the navy was unable to land me on the island that afternoon, but after stopping overnight in the sheltered harbour at Leigh, we were off Little Barrier at 6 a.m. the following morning. There was still a slight swell slopping over the large smooth slippery rocks on South Landing and I ended up with a dunking getting ashore. 28 student teachers had to be transferred quickly to the *Ngapona* before the sea conditions got too bad.

Rodger Blanshard, the ranger, and his family had been on Little Barrier since 1958 and I had first seen them on a TV documentary 'Islands of the Gulf' which had screened on NZ TV a couple of months earlier. I liked Rodger immediately and, along with his dog 'Mac', he showed me around Te Maraeroa Flat, the only area of flat land on the island. The homestead, built in the early years of the 20th century, was situated by the side of Te Waikohare Stream, then completely devoid of water. Rodger was an excellent wildlife photographer and a naturalist who expanded considerably my rather meagre knowledge of New Zealand's bird life during my stay on the Island. In those days Rodger ran a few milk cows and some sheep plus a number of chickens on the 60 odd acres of Te Maraeroa Flat. On my first night on the island I awoke in the early hours to what sounded like a distressed child crying and whimpering. I knew it couldn't be as Rodger and I were the only people on the island. This perplexing sound continued intermittently until daybreak. At breakfast I asked Rodger: "What on earth was that weird sound last night?" "Oh," he said casually, "That's the little blue penguins. They have a nest under the house!"

We began laying the concrete blocks for the new generator shed and on the second afternoon, as the weather was fine, Rodger suggested I climb to the summit of Mt Hauturu – the resting place of the winds - which is, at 2369 ft (722m), the highest point on the island. The track led through pristine, primeval forest steepening the further one got from the coast. Rodger had given me his bird-caller with which I attracted fantails and bellbirds. Further up the track I was lucky enough to see, at close hand, two stitchbirds then only found on Little Barrier, and I watched these attractive little birds for about five minutes. Andreas Reischek, the Austrian naturalist and taxidermist, also observed two stitchbirds on the island in the 1880s. His ideas of conservation were somewhat different than those of today: "(I) *saw male and female near a nest, and endeavoured to observe them unnoticed, but they quickly saw me, and in the act of escaping I shot them*." Reischek shot about 150 stitchbirds on the island – even though they were by then extinct elsewhere – on they, along with his extensive collection of over 3000 bird specimens were presented to the Imperial Natural History Museum in Vienna.

The last two or three hundred feet to the summit is through moss forest which, to the Maori, was the home of the secretive *patupaiarehe*, the forest fairies. Moss festoons the branches or forms clumps on the tree trunks in this cloud forest, giving the impression that goblins, elves or fairies must exist here. I had not experienced anything like this before. Finally I was on the summit and rain-forested valleys dropped away in all directions to the sea. I was alone on top of the world, safe in the knowledge that there was just one other person on the whole island. In the distance I could just make out Auckland and closer at hand Great Barrier Island, the Moko Hinau group, Kawau Island and the Whangaparaoa Peninsula. In those days my camera was a little Agfa Instamatic, given to me by my parents as a Christmas present the previous year, so what photos I took did not do Little Barrier justice. The descent back to Te Maraeroa Flat was certainly a lot quicker than the ascent!

The following day it began raining and it stayed that way for the last three days of my visit. The dry bed of Te Waikohare Stream soon filled up, flowing quite fast. One morning, during a break in the rain, Mac the dog suddenly began barking excitingly. Rodger looked up and immediately said it would be Fred Ladd flying over. Sure enough, breaking out of the clouds enshrouding the island's peaks, came the little TAT (Tourist Air Travel) amphibious Grumman Widgeon, skimming down over the treetops. A newspaper tumbled out, landing a few feet from the homestead, and the little plane sped off Auckland-bound. Freddy Ladd was a legend in the skies around Auckland in the 1960s, flying his little amphibious aircraft into just about every bay in the Hauraki Gulf. He was also an aspiring poet. Attached to this newspaper was a note, announcing his resignation from TAT, in his distinctive rhyming couplets:

> *Well dear folk I've got a story*
> *The whole darned thing is not of glory*
> *I resigned from TAT*
> *This I know's not good for me*
>
> *Poor old Mabel she is sad*
> *So be gone this blinking Ladd*
> *Till end of March I fly*
> *Before I leave this bit of sky.*
> *Ha! Ho!*
> *Webfooted Fred*

Fred capped off his career with TAT by flying beneath the Auckland Harbour Bridge on his last day in March 1967, much to the chagrin of the Civil Aviation and the Harbour Bridge authorities.

Chapter 2   The *Tofua* Voyage

My first foray away from New Zealand shores was, in retrospect, part of a now lost legacy. Along with my cousin, Keith, I spent my summer holiday of 1967 – 68 on a journey to the Pacific Islands on board the *Tofua*, affectionately known as the 'banana boat'. Every month this ship visited the islands of Fiji, American Samoa, Western Samoa, Niue and Tonga (both the northern island of Vava'u and the town of Nuku'alofa, the capital on Tongatapu) bringing necessary provisions to the islands, and collecting bananas, oranges, pineapples, copra, *etc.* for the New Zealand and International markets. For Niue and Vava'u, neither of which then had airfields, the monthly visit of the *Tofua* was the only regular contact the Islanders had with the outside world.

The *Tofua* left Auckland's Captain Cook Wharf on an evening in late December 1967 with all the fanfare that accompanied departing passenger ships in those days. A band was playing '*Now is the Hour*' alternating with '*Isa* Lei', the Fijian song of farewell. Coloured streamers fluttered in the breeze, stretching tightly before snapping as the ship moved away, a last fragile symbolic link between those departing and those staying; tearful relatives waved last farewells to loved ones… Yes, the departure of these ships was always an emotional experience, especially when compared with the rather impersonal departures of modern cruise liners and aircraft today.

For three days we sunbathed on the wooden deck, aware of the two pulsating Sulzer diesel engines vibrating deep below us as the *Tofua* steamed north through the calm indigo waters of the South Pacific. On the morning of New Year's Day 1968 two pure white tropic birds with long red tail-feathers appeared above the ship, a sign that we were getting close to land, and sure enough, in the early afternoon, the hazy outline of the Fijian island of Kadavu appeared on the horizon. Land Ho! This was my first sighting of a foreign land. During the afternoon we sailed along the island's coast and the distant sight of a palm-fringed shore interspersed with mainly white, red or green tin-roofed houses conjured up romantic images of Robinson Crusoe-like beachcombers, or topee-wearing colonial administrators forgotten on a torrid tropical shore. Joseph Conrad was definitely alive and well in my imagination.

That evening Keith and I walked the darkened streets of Suva, both of us putting our feet on a foreign shore for the first time. The next morning, I purchased my first SLR camera, a Ricoh Singlex, which was to serve me well for many years. In the afternoon we set out on a local tour of the environs of Suva during which we visited a small mosque. At the time the tenets of Islam were completely unknown to me; I believed the mosque was something like a pagan temple and this was my first taste of the exotic 'East', even if it was in the heart of the South Pacific.

I had been looking forward to the *Tofua*'s next port. This was Apia in what was then Western Samoa, and it was here that my grandparents had spent the first years of their married life. Unfortunately, I had no information as to where my great-grandfather, George Westbrook's trading store was located and had no contacts of any distant relatives who may have still resided on the Island. I did know that most of them had already moved to New Zealand. Samoa didn't disappoint. I became enamoured with the paradisiacal beauty of the islands although, in places, this was somewhat tarnished by the overwater privies which then lined the coastline just out of Apia. With an improved sewage system, these have now been removed. In 1968 Robert Louis Stevenson's house at Vailima was the Samoan head of state's residence but we were able to visit the wondrous gardens, my introduction to colourful tropical flora. During our tour we spent time in an idyllic sun-warmed pool at the base of a waterfall surrounded by the lush vegetation endemic to the tropics.

In a small village near Apia, we were entertained by the local Cultural group and it was here, for the first time, I tasted kava, or *'ava* in Samoan, the traditional ceremonial drink of welcome made from the root of the *Piper methysticum* plant. This drink is mildly narcotic rather than alcoholic and, although interesting, I didn't find the taste particularly pleasing to my then rather conservative palate. It looked like dishwater and tasted like peppery dishwater! The traditional way kava, or *yaqona* as it is called in Fiji, was prepared was by chewing pieces of the kava root and spitting the semimasticated fibres into a special wooden receptacle known as a *tanoa.* Water was added and a strainer, made from hibiscus bark, was used for straining the woody root fibres. The drink is then served in special cups of polished half-coconut shells. To cater for modern day European sensibilities, the root is now pounded rather than chewed, much to our relief. To a kava connoisseur, however, the traditional saliva-activated beverage is by far the better!

When we left Apia, the famous Samoan hotelier Aggie Grey boarded the *Tofua* to travel to Auckland. An excited dance troupe performed on the wharf to farewell her. In the past there had been hearsay rumours that Aggie had been the model for both James Michener's Bloody Mary in *Tales of the South Pacific* and Sadie Thompson in Somerset Maugham's *Rain* but neither of these rumours were ever substantiated and both highly unlikely. With regards to Somerset Maugham, he visited the Samoas well before Aggie's time. Aggie had established Aggie Grey's Hotel in Apia in 1933 and, during World War Two, it had catered for American servicemen stationed in Samoa. It has been a popular institution ever since. Keith and I visited the hotel bar during our time in Apia.

Our next port of call was Pago Pago on the island of Tutuila and capital of American Samoa. This is, perhaps, the best deep-water harbour in the Pacific, and is dominated by Rainmaker Mountain which lived up to its name. The town is one of the wettest in the Pacific and was the inspiration of a short story by Somerset Maugham, appropriately called *Rain,* written in 1920: *"It was not like our soft English rain that drops gently on the earth; it was unmerciful and somehow terrible; you felt in it the malignancy of the primitive powers of nature. It did not pour, it flowed."*

One of the world's longest single-span cable-cars, built a couple of years earlier to service a TV transmitter, trundled across the harbour and up Mt Alava but unfortunately, for unknown reasons, was not operating on the day of our visit.

The *Tofua* arrived in Pago Pago about the same time as the American cruise ship *Mariposa* operated by Matson Lines which, along with its sister-ship *Monterey*, regularly sailed to New Zealand and Australia via the Pacific Islands. Our ship was moored close to the Intercontinental Hotel and we were able to use the hotel swimming pool as a welcome relief from the hot muggy tropical heat. During the morning, we walked along a surprisingly vehicle-clogged road to a park in central Pago Pago to watch as a belated Father Christmas (who had arrived on the *Mariposa*) distributed presents to a large gathering of excited Samoan children.

The following morning, I awoke with a start. Sunlight was streaming through the porthole and all seemed silent. The ship's engines had stopped and every so often there was a loud metallic clunk. I could hear muffled shouts and laughter. On peering through our cabin porthole, I could see a low palm-covered shore from which a number of small lighters were approaching. I could see people, some slowly making their way to the small coastal settlement, others just standing around watching the ship. We were anchored off Alofi, the main town on the small island of Niue. In the 1960s the *Tofua* was the only regular contact Niue had with the outside world. 'Ship Day' was a day when the islanders brought their shell and seed necklaces, woven palm-leaved hats and baskets to sell in the small open-air market and the kids spent their pocket money on the short-lived supply of Tip Top ice cream the ship had brought from New Zealand. Supplies of butter, powdered milk, tinned bully-beef and other essential foodstuffs were replenished in the Island's stores.

Keith and I went up on deck to watch the unloading proceedings. Several lighters were milling around the ship, their crew, in the carefree Polynesian way, were splashing each other with their oars or throwing lumps of ice, retrieved from the ship's refrigerated hold, at each other. One lighter was resting alongside the ship, unknowingly under the bilge outlet, the pump of which had been turned off. Suddenly the pump spluttered into life, flooding water into the boat, much to the delight and laughter of other crews. The afflicted crew, laughing loudly, began furiously bailing using coconut halves carried for such an eventuality. A small truck had been unloaded with the ship's derrick onto a raft and was now being towed ashore. All cargo and passengers had to be taken ashore by lighter as the small wharf on the island did not extend as far as the island's barrier reef. A Niuean in an outrigger was fishing near the stern of the ship. When asked what he used for bait, he indicated coconut flesh: *"Coconut! That's no good. How do you expect to catch fish with coconut?"* He spoke limited English, chattering away, mainly to himself, in the local Polynesian language until his fishing line became entangled on a coral outcrop below. It became evident that the Niuean language does not have the same extensive vocabulary of colourful expletives as English!

Before we went ashore we had to wait while a Datsun Bluebird car, owned by the new school teacher who was disembarking with his family, was unloaded onto a raft. One of the Niuean stevedores found that the car was unlocked and that the horn worked. We followed the raft ashore in one of the lighters, to the accompaniment of continual horn-beeping and the laughter of the crew, much to the consternation of the teacher's two small children who were in our lighter and becoming increasingly upset. Bill, our cabin mate, had gifts from a Niuean work-mate in Auckland for his family on the island, and we were able to find them in the local market at Alofi. It was my first experience of the hospitality of the Pacific Islanders. We were invited to share a snack of boiled taro, kumara, cooked mussels still frozen from the ship and bully beef washed down with fresh coconut water straight from the nut, all the while squatting in the shade of a corrugated iron shed in the market. There was little in the market for us to buy, just a few shell necklaces, bead bangles, woven palm-leaf hats and baskets. I heard later that Aggie Grey, had bought up most of the Islanders' handicrafts to sell in her shop in Auckland, much to the annoyance of other passengers. We spent part of the afternoon swimming in the warm tropical waters off the coralline coast with some of the local Niuean children, buying them ice creams before we re-embarked mid-afternoon, setting off for the Tongan islands.

I was on deck early the next morning as we steamed through the stunning islands of the Vava'u Archipelago. The surface of the sea was mirror-like as we passed the Belfast-registered copra ship *Beaverbank*, resting idly at anchor in a placid bay near the main town of Neiafu. Later that morning we travelled by launch to the stunningly beautiful 'Anapekapeka, or Swallows Cave on Kapa Island. At night thousands of swiflets nest in this cave but none were evident during our visit, however a pleasant morning was spent swimming in the deep, clear water from the old launch before we returned to the tiny settlement of Neiafu. At lunchtime a heavy rainstorm lashed the little town and the streets were still wet when we wandered down the main street to the Burns Philp general store, a focal point of almost every settlement in the islands of the South Pacific.

The *Tofua* left Vava'u mid-afternoon amid much good-natured hilarity. Like Niue, Vava'u did not have an airfield and the *Tofua* was the island group's only regular contact with the outside world and anyone leaving the island to travel to Nuku'alofa, the Tongan capital, had to do so by boat. The *Tofua* would accommodate local interisland travellers on the deck. A late-comer, a rather large Tongan lady and her children arrived just as the ship was beginning to move away from the dock. The captain, seeing the late-comer, held the ship, now untethered, close to the wharf under engine power. Helped by an enthusiastically jovial crowd, the woman, with some physical assistance, was pushed through a lower porthole, following her two more agile children. As the ship backed away from the wharf, we began to see men leaping over the bow. Evidently this was a fun local ritual where the local stevedores remained on board until the ship began backing away. They then leapt or dived overboard, to the great delight of the crowd, and swam back to the wharf. No health and safety in those days!

That evening we spent time in the wheelhouse along with the ship's officers looking for a volcano in the Metis Shoal off Tofua, the ship's namesake island. On the ship's previous voyage in December the crew had seen and reported the eruption of an underwater volcano which had created an island of considerable height and this was what we were hoping to see. Unfortunately, we were to be disappointed. Volcanic activity had ceased and the loose volcanic debris – scoria and pumice – had been eroded away by the actions of the tropical seas during the intervening month. All that was left now was a low 'sand' bank, visible only on the ship's radar.

In Nuku'alofa, Keith and I were shown the highlights of Tongatapu by a penfriend with whom I had corresponded for a couple of years. We visited the enigmatic Ha'amonga a Maui, a large trilithon constructed by the 11th Tu'i Tonga in the 13th century, the Flying foxes (fruit bats) of Kolovai and the Mapu'a a Vaca blowholes on the south coast of the island. Our visit to Nuku'alofa culminated that evening in a visit to a local cinema to see a double-feature – the classic 1949 Humphrey Bogart movie 'Knock on Any Door' and the 1962 psychological thriller 'What Ever Happened to Baby Jane?' starring Bette Davis and Joan Crawford. A rather incongruous ending to our visit to the Kingdom of Tonga! The ship sailed in the early hours of the morning heading back to Suva, before proceeding on to Auckland.

Next morning, as the Tongan Islands fell behind us, we lay on deck listening to a local radio station playing the full recording of the Beatles *Sgt Peppers Lonely Heart Club Band,* the album having been released just a few months earlier. It was the first time I had heard the full recording. The rest of the voyage passed pleasantly enough. The *Tofua* was not an uncomfortable vessel to travel on and although there was no swimming pool, there was plenty of space to sunbathe. We would often see Aggie Grey sitting on deck with her male companion. She would always smile pleasantly and nod in acknowledgement when we passed. The *Tofua* arrived back at Captain Cook Wharf early on a January morning, pushed into her berth by the old Auckland Harbour tug *Te Awhina.*

For me the voyage on the *Tofua* had been an enjoyable introduction to international travel and I was smitten by the travel bug, although it would be another two years before I was off on my first real Overseas Experience. In the meantime, it was back to clerical life at the Department of Lands & Survey in Auckland.

There is something exciting about seeing a foreign land for the first time. On New Years Day 1968 I sighted the island of Kadavu in Fiji from the deck of the MV *Tofua*.

MV *Tofua* off the wharf at Alofi on the island of Niue, January 1968

Chapter 3   Return to Little Barrier

One day at the end of April 1968 I was again called into the office of Darcy O'Brien who was now Commissioner of Crown Lands for the Auckland Region, and asked if I would like to go again to Little Barrier Island – the next day! This time it was to help move Rodger Blanshard and his family off the island and the new ranger, John Wisnesky and his wife Betty, onto the island. Rodger had a new position as head ranger of the newly created Hauraki Gulf Maritime Park and would now be based on Kawau Island.

I left Auckland on the MV *Colville*, the last of the Great Barrier Island whale-chasers which now regularly serviced the outer islands and the manned lighthouses of the Hauraki Gulf. The *Colville* arrived off Little Barrier early the same afternoon and after the Wisnesky's horse was coaxed overboard and swum ashore, we began to unload their household possessions which took about two hours. The *Colville* then left us, heading to Cuvier and Moko Hinau Islands, and would be back at Little Barrier in a couple of days. In the interim, we would move all the Blanshards' personal effects and household furniture into the boathouse on South Landing for easier loading when the *Colville* returned. We all prayed that the weather would hold good and that a south-westerly wind would not spring up.

While we waited for the return of the *Colville*, I had some spare time and having my new Ricoh with me, was able to take much better photographs than I had on my previous visit to the island. Each morning the forest parrots, or kaka would come down to the troughs in the garden near the ranger's house in which was placed sugared water as an artificial nectar. The kaka would be joined by olive-green bellbirds and the white-bibbed tui. The garden echoed with a cacophony of mellifluous birdsong, and I was able to take my first photos of New Zealand's unique birdlife.

I spent the afternoon, first scrambling along the dry, rain-forest enshrouded Te Waikohare Stream, before wandering across Te Maraeroa Flat and through Pua Mataahu, a sacred pohutukawa grove, where two Maori tribes had fought a furious battle three centuries earlier. Te Maraeroa Flat culminates in the apex of Te Titoki Point with three distinctive old gnarled pohutukawa trees, each side of which there are notorious boulder beaches. I stood on the point and looked back along the South Landing towards the only cluster of buildings on the Island. This is the main landing on Little Barrier and an advisory, given to those permitted to land on the island, states: '*Landing is by way of a boulder beach and often through surf. It is usually impossible to avoid getting wet.*' Looking the other way, I could see the even more difficult, and little used, West Landing and the steep rugged cliffs of Haowhenua beyond. Behind Te Maraeroa Flat the island rose up in a series of dense rain forested ridges to the summit of Mt Hauturu. This certainly was a primeval wilderness, often claimed to be what mainland New Zealand was like before the arrival of the genus *homo* sapiens about a thousand years ago. It was in a thoughtful mood that I strolled back, disturbing a few sheep grazing among a tangle of *Muehlenbeckia* scrub, to the house where Ann, Rodger's wife was preparing the evening meal. Later that evening I went out kiwi hunting with Ann, Susi - the youngest Blanshard daughter, and a zoology student. After several abortive attempts to corner the quickly moving birds, Susi finally shouted that she had one. She carefully held the two feet together as kiwis have rather sharp claws which can cause nasty gashes. I was amazed at how soft the feathers were, just like down. This was the first time I had seen a live kiwi up close, let alone touched one. It was a very special experience.

When the *Colville* returned we loaded the Blanshard's household effects in about an hour and a half and headed off to Mansion House Bay on Kawau Island. En route the *Colville* tied alongside the *Florence Kennedy* off Flat Rock to take on more stores for the lighthouse keepers at Moko Hinau. Flat Rock was often mistaken for a distant ship when seen from our Army Bay bach, and we could see its lonely winking light at night, so I found it interesting to view and photograph this beacon at close quarters.

At Mansion House Bay, it took us about two and half hours to unload and transfer the Blanshard's household furniture to their new quarters on Kawau. I had been booked into the Mansion House itself for the night. This historic building was built between 1845 and 1847 as the residence for the coppermine superintendent on the island and was acquired by Governor Sir George Grey in 1862. Grey then expanded the house and planted extensive exotic gardens. He also introduced several exotic birds and animals, including monkeys and even a couple of zebra, of which just the kookaburras, peacocks and the wallabies remained. In 1968 the Mansion House was in its last days as an up-market hotel that had been particularly popular with honeymooners, but plans were already afoot for its closure. I spent time after dinner, over a rum and coke in the darkened bar, discussing the future of the hotel with the Dutch barman. I felt quite privileged to have stayed there. The Mansion House has now been restored to its condition at the time of Grey's tenure and is now open as a museum only. Next morning, I was met at Sandspit wharf, on the mainland, by a colleague and on our way back to Auckland we were stopped and had our footwear and vehicle checked over by Ministry of Agriculture staff. This was not long after a serious Foot and Mouth outbreak had occurred in the UK, and the Ministry was conducting an exercise just in case there should be an similar outbreak of the disease in New Zealand.

Less than a month later I was again summoned to Darcy O'Brien's office. This time I was asked if I would be prepared to go to Hen Island to assist in the search for a 'shipwrecked' cat. This was certainly something a little different, so again I jumped at the opportunity.

Taranga, or Hen Island, is the largest of the Hen & Chickens island group off the Northland coast. The islands were named by Captain Cook who thought Taranga looked like a broody hen and the six smaller islands her miscreant chickens. Like Little Barrier, the Hen & Chickens also have the special status of a wildlife sanctuary with restricted access. In pre-European days, the island had been occupied by a local Maori tribe, the Ngatiwai, who had cultivated a small section of the island, leaving behind as evidence, the remains of stone walls and a population of the kiore, or Polynesian rats – *rattus exulans*. We would, however, be camping in the rainforest at the opposite, less hospitable, end of the island. In 1968 the island was the last refuge of the North Island saddleback, or *tieke*, a critically endangered New Zealand wattle-bird and this was the reason why it was so important to find the cat.

I was driven up to Whangarei where, along with Rodger Blanshard and Graham Adams of the Wildlife Division of the Internal Affairs Department, we were briefed by Police sergeant Paddy McDonnell on what was known of the wreck of the trimaran *Kotuku*. The circumstances of the wreck were subject to query, but it appeared that the *Kotuku* with six people on board, and a cat, had hit the rocks on the western coast of Hen Island. The crew had been marooned on the island for a week before they were rescued. Of concern to the Lands and Survey and the Wildlife Departments was the fate of 'Simon', the trimaran's cat. The castaways had conflicting accounts as to what had happened to Simon although they all seemed to think that he was dead. Our job was to look for any traces of the cat – dead birds, rats, *etc.* – and to lay traps in case any European rats had got ashore as these would be equally devastating to the *tieke* population. The European rats are larger and more voracious than the smaller *kiore*, which had arrived during the pre-European Maori occupation of the Island. The kiore have since been eradicated from the Hen & Chickens.

We were taken out to Hen Island by the Fisheries Protection launch *Ohorere* and after scrambling ashore on the rocky eastern coast, we set up a bush camp some 20 metres above the shore. To reach the wreck we had to scramble up, through trackless bush, and over a ridge about 200 metres high then descend, precariously, down a makeshift path that in places was almost vertical. This was made worse as we were all lugging cat traps on our backs which tended to catch on every low branch or supplejack vine. We eventually reached the wreck of the *Kotuku* which was now badly broken up by the action of the sea. Cans of food and other debris were strewn for some distance on each side of the wreck. We set the cat and some rat traps in the forest in the vicinity of the wreck and inspected the wreckage before making our way back over the ridge to our camp.

Our camp was, in effect, just a couple of tent flies stretched between trees in the dense bush. This gave us some protection against any rain that might fall, and we did have some. We cooked under one fly and slept under the other. There was a track of sorts that passed through the camp and we found out what used it when, on the first night, a little blue penguin waddled between our sleeping-bags, protesting noisily when Paddy rolled on it. Petrels also nested in this area of forest and we caught two as they dropped through the forest canopy in search of their burrows. One was a common grey-faced petrel and the other, a smaller, prettier bird Graham identified as a rare Pycroft's petrel. The next day we set further rat and cat traps along the ridge and on checking those we had set the previous day both at the wreck and on the ridge, found only *kiore*. No sign of Simon the cat was ever found, so he obviously never made it ashore.

One afternoon I had a little time on the Hen for some private contemplation in the island's rainforest and found a moss-covered boulder to sit upon. I could hear, muffled by the coastal pohutukawa trees, the blue waters of the Pacific murmuring around the jagged coastal rocks. The leaves of the taraire trees above swayed gently in the soft cool breeze. An inquisitive fantail flitted and swooped around me before heading off into the darker recesses of the bush in its quest for insects. Two kakariki, the little red-capped bright green parakeets, noisily attacked the fruit of a nearby karaka tree and in the distance I could hear the raucous screech of a kaka, the forest parrot. A fat kereru, the New Zealand pigeon, swooped past with a whooshing of wings and an invisible bellbird sang three clear resonant notes, then all was silent. The glade I was sitting in was cool with the broken winter's sunlight filtering through the upper canopy.

Behind me the steep rock face was covered with an entanglement of supplejack vines, the climbing, pandanus-related kiekie and the nasty hooked bush lawyer, a New Zealand native of the blackberry family. I was alone in this virgin wilderness. This was the New Zealand rainforest before the arrival of the Polynesians and I felt privileged to be able to relax and enjoy its primeval solitude. As I made my way back to our encampment I was excited to observe a *tieke* feeding unconcernedly in the leaf-litter quite close to me. I watched it for some time and could see how easily this attractive bird could fall prey to a voracious 'shipwrecked' cat.

On our last day on the island, after collecting all the traps, we set fire to what was left of the trimaran, destroying all traces of the wreck, before being picked up by the Northland Harbour Board tug *Ngapuhi* and taken back to Whangarei. For me it had been quite an experience. It was the first time I had camped in the real New Zealand rainforest and even though it was early June, the weather on the island hadn't been too bad, just a little rain and some wind. When I arrived back at the Lands & Survey office I was handed a note from Rodger Blanshard who, due to pressing duties in his role as head ranger of the Hauraki Gulf Maritime Park, had had to leave Hen Island several days before us:

Dear Neil,
Just a note to thank you for your willing help and co-operation in "operation Simon" at Hen

Island under such atrocious conditions. If the weather over the weekend here is any indication of what you had to put up with I can't say how sorry I felt for you up on the island. I can only say that I hope you managed to catch Simon in order to justify the effort, and that in the few fine spells you managed to see some birds and a good photo or two to remember the island. I hope you got home safely and without having caught a cold or other ill.

So until I next see you in the office will wish you all the very best and thank you once more.
    Yours sincerely
    Rodger Blanshard

The island had obviously escaped the worst of the weather that Rodger had described!

My time with the Lands & Survey was now coming to an end with the pull of overseas travel becoming stronger. In November 1968 I moved to a mundane accounts job with Air New Zealand out at the Auckland International Airport, mainly for the perk of subsidised flights. At the end of 1969 I took my mother to Fiji for a week. This was the first time she had been out of New Zealand and she enjoyed it. I had, by then, already made plans to head Overland through Asia to England and so this Fijian interlude was really a restful holiday where we spent time at a resort at Korolevu on the Coral Coast and a couple of days at Vuda Point near Lautoka before returning to Auckland.

My decision to travel Overland to Britain from Kathmandu had been partly fueled by a similar journey made by a work colleague a couple of years earlier. I had also attended a slide presentation by Tim Round, hosted by Atlantic & Pacific Travel in Auckland. Tim was a popular tour guide, well-known in New Zealand for many years for his escorted tours to off-beat places. Shortly thereafter I booked my trip. The cost of the land journey was then NZ$325.00 and the flight from Singapore via Bangkok to Kathmandu was NZ$105.00. As I was working for Air New Zealand I could get a staff concession for the flight from Auckland to Singapore. In those days the thought of travel across Asia, particularly through India, was alien to most people and many queried my sanity. An English work colleague couldn't quite understand why I would spend over $300 getting to UK 'the slow way', when he was travelling to Southampton on the Russian ship *Shota Rustaveli* for only NZ$150. The only stop his ship would make between NZ and the UK was at Panama but "there'd be plenty of chicks on board". My priorities for travelling were a little different than his!

Christmas 1969 and New Year 1970 were memorable in that it was the last time I spent with friends from my formative teenage years, particularly friendships I had formed during my time with the Lands & Survey. One or two had married and several were planning to take the big step in the near future. My parents held what was virtually an open house at the family bach at Army Bay. Friends came and went all through the Christmas period and there was a big party on New Year's Eve. The weather couldn't have been better, and many a bottle of DB and Lion Red was consumed. It was the end of my life in what was then still a fairly parochial New Zealand and I was now stepping out into the big wide world – an innocent abroad!

The original homestead on Little Barrier Island, a restricted wildlife sanctuary in the Hauraki Gulf. May 1968

Before we left Hen Island we fired the remains of the wreck of the trimaran *Kotuku*. June 1968

Chapter 4   Auckland to Kathmandu

It was a fine February morning in 1970 when I flew out of Auckland International Airport. Asia and, ultimately, the UK were beckoning. I was flying first to Singapore and then onwards to Kathmandu to join a Penn Overland tour. I can remember, as the Air New Zealand DC-8 climbed steadily westwards, looking out of the window and seeing far below a white trail left by a farmer as he spread phosphates on the green fields of the Awhitu Peninsula far below. With tears in my eyes I wondered when I would next see my homeland, family and friends, but the wide world called and as the white-lined Tasman coastline dropped away my thoughts turned to the journey and adventures that lay ahead.

I arrived in Singapore on the eve of the Chinese New Year, the Year of the Dog, and in the narrow streets of Chinatown where my hotel, the Seventh Story, was situated things were beginning to heat up. Singapore in 1970 was quite different to the modern metropolis of today. Much of the original Chinatown was then still intact. Construction of the tall buildings that now characterise this city state had not yet begun. On the evening of my arrival the narrow streets were a hive of activity with dragon dancers and their entourage, weaving in and out and around the colonnaded businesses below, accompanied by the inevitable fireworks. I watched it all from the upstairs windows in the hotel restaurant. The bangs and blasts increased in intensity as the evening progressed and at one stage, two American sailors who were staying at the hotel, suddenly dived to the floor of the restaurant after one particularly loud explosion. They said they were on 'R & R' from Vietnam and it was just a spontaneous reaction to an explosion, but I suspect it may have just been done for effect!

To a young man used to the rather conservative way of life in Auckland in the late 1960s, Singapore was an eye-opener. It was the first time I had experienced life at its core. Shops sold everything, and the range of merchandise was to me astounding. There were specialists; one street just seemed to be full of steel tubing, in another were metal forgers. Empty 44-gallon drums were on sale, old used vehicle engines were being stripped down on the street and the parts sold. A coffin-maker in a street near the hotel particularly intrigued me. The rather elaborate coffins illustrated the importance of death and the afterlife to the Chinese Singaporeans. I wandered the streets, becoming used to the hustle and bustle, to the smells of small local restaurants and the hawkers' stalls. I experienced strange foods, food I would not have even considered trying before I left home. Today much of this food is now commonplace in Auckland. On my third night in Singapore I was invited to a meal by the friend of a Chinese colleague of mine at Air New Zealand. This was a 'steamboat', a Chinese hot pot very popular in Singapore. The soup-like stock was cooked at the table over a portable butane burner and various ingredients were added during the course of the evening. Meats were followed by vegetables then seafood. I struggled with chopsticks during the course of the meal but fortunately a fork was also provided. This was my first truly exotic meal and I baulked a little at some of the ingredients, mainly because I didn't know what they were. I noted in my diary that additions to the soup '*included several types of fish, cuttlefish tentacles, cockles, prawns, fish balls – which were very strong,* (at least I thought so then) – *pig livers, quails' eggs and chicken gizzards, amongst other things*.' Michael, my host, seemed to take great delight in giving me various titbits then telling me what they were. A couple of nights later I was invited to the home of a Chinese optician, another friend of my Air New Zealand colleague to whom I had delivered some duty-free goods. Here we had a more conventional Chinese meal which I greatly enjoyed.

On one afternoon, I took a tour to Johore Bahru, just across the Causeway in Malaysia. The tour visited the Gardens of Istana Besar and the Sultan Abu Bakar State Mosque and on our way back into Singapore we stopped at the thought-provoking Kranji War Memorial and Cemetery for the Commonwealth soldiers who had died during the Japanese invasion and occupation in World War Two. On another day, I visited Singapore's Botanical Gardens where I came upon wild monkeys for the first time. I spent an afternoon in the famous Tiger Balm, or Haw Par Villa, Gardens with its brightly coloured statues of characters from Chinese mythology. I was particularly intrigued with the Ten Courts of Hell and its graphic dioramas. I wrote home in a letter: "*One grotto deals with the ten halls of Hell and has some of the most gruesome scenes I have seen; unfortunate beings being disembowelled, crushed, thrown into boiling cauldrons, cut in half at the waist; one unfortunate had even been strapped in a kneeling position while two devils were cutting him in half from the head down with a crosscut saw!*"

After a week, it was time to leave Singapore for Kathmandu, capital of the Kingdom of Nepal, where my Overland journey was to begin. The flight to Kathmandu included an overnight stop in Bangkok, then a vibrant city catering mainly to the sexual needs of the American servicemen embroiled in the debacle of the Vietnam War. I was in transit for only a few hours in Bangkok, just enough for a few hours' sleep at a hotel and consequently I did not see anything of the Thai capital in the daylight. The Thai Airlines flight to Kathmandu was by way of Calcutta and the flight path took the aircraft right over Rangoon. From the air the glimmering golden spire of the Shwe Dagon Pagoda could be seen quite clearly far below. After a brief stop at Dum Dum airport in Calcutta we approached the high peaks of the Himalayas. Kanchenjunga and also Everest were sighted before the aircraft banked steeply and dropped down into the Kathmandu Valley on the approaches to Tribhuvan International Airport.

If Singapore was my introductory culture shock, Kathmandu was the ultimate. I noted in my diary at the time that it was like being transported back to '*medieval days*'. Other travellers I have spoken to who visited Kathmandu in the 60s and 70s felt the same way. In 1970 Nepal was still a mysterious kingdom high in the Himalayas which few people visited, hippies excepted. Of course, there was the connection with New Zealand through the work of Sir Edmund Hillary in the construction of schools in the remote Himalayan foothills. Mahendra was king and Kathmandu was the end of the so-called hippy trail which ran across Asia from Europe. The country had only opened up to visitors in the early 1960s some years after the first road over the mountains from India, the Tribhuvan Rajpath, had been constructed. In February 1970 the Hetauda to Kathmandu Ropeway carried the bulk of goods up to Kathmandu from India and there was still a Government hashish shop from where the pernicious weed could be purchased legally. The aptly named 'Freak' Street was buzzing with Nepalese … and with hippies. Kathmandu was then the ultimate destination.

Although I visited Kathmandu many times in later years it was this first visit, this first impression, which was the most memorable. On that first afternoon I walked through Thamel and into Durbar Square. Old wooden and brick buildings lurched crazily over narrow streets. Ancient temples – Buddhist and Hindu – existed side by side with the images of gods and goddesses, some abnormally fierce with glaring eyes staring frighteningly at passers-by. Newaris, Tibetans, Sherpas, Indians all intermingled in a mélange that fascinated me. There was very little motorised traffic, the bulk of the non-pedestrian transport being bicycles and bicycle-rickshaws and even they, at times, could make very little progress through the milling pedestrian crowds. A flute seller tried to tempt me with his bamboo flutes while a labourer pushed past with a great stack of partially cured hides on his back. Kathmandu was the first place I encountered the ubiquitous street beggars with the children being particularly persistent. It was also the first place that I had seen homeless people sleeping in the street. As I walked back to the hotel one night I came across a young boy and girl, presumably brother and sister of no more than 5 or 6, asleep on the pavement under a covering of old sacks with their dog snuggled up beside them. It was a heart-breaking scene when seen for the first time.

Over the next few days I explored Kathmandu, accompanied by members from the Overland group I was joining. Life in the back streets was particularly fascinating, once you got use to the fact that many residents urinated and defecated in the drains and performed their daily ablutions quite openly. Women washed clothes, or their hair, under roadside hand pumps, completely oblivious to the children playing, the dogs and chickens fossicking and the passers-by going about their other business. Basic shoulder-yokes were commonly used for carrying baskets, pails and water cans, *etc*. Freak Street, or *Jhhonchen Tole* to use the Nepalese name, was the centre of Western hippy culture in Kathmandu. Small shops, cheap hotels, seedy bars and dope dens, had gained it a notorious reputation over the years and the more refined travellers tended to avoid the area, particularly at night.

In a cluster of ramshackle buildings near Durbar Square is the unobtrusive Palace of Kumari Ghar, the Living Goddess. Kumari means 'virgin' in both Nepali and Sanskrit and a little girl, the Living Goddess, is believed to be an incarnation of Taleju, another name for the Hindu warrior goddess Durga. Reminiscent of a vestal virgin of ancient Rome, this little girl is selected esoterically by Buddhist priests through a series of stringent tests, which show the close association between the Buddhists and Hindus in Nepal. In her final test, the little girl must spend a night alone in a room with the heads of ritually slaughtered goats and buffaloes without showing fear. Except for the ten days of the annual chariot festival the Kumari, or living goddess, is confined to her palace with a woman guardian seeing to all her needs and performing the maternal role. Her family can visit rarely, if at all. As soon as the Kumari shows signs of pubescence and with the onset of menstruation, a new virgin is selected and the current Kumari returns to her family. On my visit in 1970 the Kumari was a pretty little girl of about 5 years old. Clad in a scarlet robe, her hair tied in a topknot with a scarlet ribbon, her brow overlaid with vermilion paste upon which was painted the *agni chakchuu*, or fire eye, a symbol of her special powers of perception. Her striking little eyes were outlined in the traditional kohl, or lamp black. She appeared briefly on a balcony looking down benignly on me and my companion with the wide-eyed innocence of the young, before being ushered into another room, out of sight. Her appearance created little disturbance among the other ladies in the grubby courtyard, one washing clothes in a soapy bowl, another searching for nits in her daughter's hair.

On a hill overlooking Kathmandu city is Swayambhunath Stupa, also known as the Monkey Temple. A long flight of stairs leads to this magnificent structure, a large golden stupa dating from the 5th century AD. Painted upon each of the four sides of the main stupa are the eyes of the Buddha. These glaring eyes are symbolic of Buddha's all-pervading presence. In place of a nose there is a representation of the number one in the Nepali alphabet, signifying that the single way to enlightenment is via the Vajrayana path of Buddhism prevalent in Nepal. The third eye, signifying the wisdom of looking within, is depicted on the forehead between the two eyes and no ears are shown as it is said the Buddha is not interested in hearing prayers in praise of himself. Surrounding the Golden Temple are numerous shrines, chaityas or small stupas, Tantric statues, prayer wheels, Shiva lingams, and a large Vajra or sacred thunderbolt, symbol of the Vajrana form of Buddhism. There is a Hindu temple to Harati, Goddess of smallpox which signifies the intermingling of Hinduism and Buddhism; Buddhists have no incarnation in their own pantheon to protect against the dreaded smallpox, so they have adopted the Hindu deity for protection. Langur monkeys have free reign here, hence Swayambhunath is often referred to by Westerners as the 'Monkey Temple'.

The legend of the origin of Swayambhunath is rather beautiful. Once upon a time the Kathmandu Valley was a vast lake from which grew a lotus. The valley became known as 'Swayambhu', the self-created. After seeing a vision of a lotus, the Bodhisattva Manjushri travelled to Swayambhu to worship the lotus. He saw that the valley would make a good place for settlement, so he cut a gorge through the mountains through which the water drained. The lotus became the hill, the flower became the golden Swayambhunath Stupa and the drained lake became the fertile Kathmandu Valley now made suitable for human habitation. With a companion I struggled to the top of the stairs, avoiding the squabbling monkeys clamouring for food. Swayambhunath is a serene retreat, certainly a place of peace after the hustle and bustle of downtown Kathmandu. Many Tibetans, refugees from their homeland not so very far away across the mountains, come here to pray and to spin the numerous prayer wheels.

During my stay in Kathmandu I hired a bicycle, so was able to range further from the city centre and it was on one of these excursions that I met my first *sadhu,* or holyman, at a delightful little Hindu temple at Buddhanilkanth. He sat, serenely in meditation, in front of a small wood fire in a small cell and allowed me to take his photo. Outside women devotees placed marigolds in the pool of the Reclining Vishnu. Vishnu is one of the major gods of the Hindu Trimurti, or Trinity. I knew very little about the complexities of the Hindu religion in those days, but soon learnt that the Hindu trinity was made up of the major gods Brahma, the creator, Vishnu the preserver and Shiva, the destroyer. To complicate things, each of these deities have many manifestations all known by different names, as do their consorts, Sarasvati, Lakshmi and Parvati. All the above 'gods' are an aspect of Brahman, the Absolute, - *'neither good nor evil, the source of all things'*. It was to take quite a few trips to India for me to even begin to understand the rudiments of this fascinating religion.

Further away from the city, in the heart of the rural Kathmandu Valley, is the largest and most important Buddhist shrine in the Valley. This is Bodhnath Stupa, the most sacred shrine of Buddhists in Nepal and, like Swayambhunath, has a large Tibetan community living in its vicinity. The bowl of the Stupa is larger than Swayambhunath and the golden tower is stepped in pyramid fashion with hundreds of prayer flags fluttering in the breeze. Like Swayambhunath, the all-seeing eyes of the Buddha glare out from all four sides of the stupa. At Bodhnath I had an audience with the 3rd Chini Lama, the head Lama of all Nepal. The Chini Lama was once powerful in the temporal affairs of Nepal, but as a result of modernisation, his influence was now purely religious. While I remember that he was worldly wise, I can remember very little of our conversation. I did hear later that he was regarded as a bit of a rogue, a known liar and cheat who had spent time in prison for illegal money dealings. While I was with him he passed on a globule of opium to a couple of hippies then told me how evil the stuff was!

Bodhnath is surrounded by richly cultivated fields, which I had cycled through on my journey from the city, passing through some impressive areas of rice terracing. I noticed many of the rural dwellings had walls covered with cow dung and straw patties drying in the sun for future use as fuel, and saw a number of women making these patties, *'up to their elbows in the filthy, stinking mixture of cow shit and straw.'*

I returned to Kathmandu via Pashupatinath, the site on the Bagmati River where the local Hindu residents are cremated after death. This is the most important Hindu temple to the god Shiva in Nepal and is a huge complex of small shrines and temples. Only Hindus born in Nepal or India can enter the main complex. I was able to view the temple from the opposite bank of the Bagmati. Near the entrance I came across a group of sadhus, wild looking characters sitting on a bench. The wildest of them approached me and to my surprise, in a very cultured English voice asked me from where I came. He surprised me by knowing quite a lot about New Zealand.

It was now time to leave Kathmandu with Penn Overland. Our tour leader was Hubert Decleer, a Belgian who in later years became an international authority in Tibetan studies, translating many Tibetan Buddhist manuscripts and lecturing in Europe and America at

University level on the Tibetan and Nepalese cultures. Hubert was assisted by his wife Maritza and their little white dog 'Moti' would accompany us. Our group left Kathmandu in two local buses for the journey over the Tribhuvan Rajpath to the border town of Birganj. In 1970 this was the only land connection with India; the Prithvi Highway, via Pokhara, was opened a few years later. Our buses slowly wound up through the foothills, stopping at the small village of Daman where we had lunch at the Everest Point Restaurant. There are dramatic views of the Himalayas but unfortunately Mt Everest, which can be seen clearly from here, was hidden in the clouds. We did, however, have fine views of Machhapuchhre or Fish Tail Peak, in the Annapurna Himal.

It was after dark when we finally reached the small Samjhana hotel in Birganj, said to be the worst on the whole Overland and, on reflection, I had no reason to dispute that fact. Even now I shudder when I recall the one broken toilet at the hotel that had to service two bus groups of close to 90 people!

I was intrigued by these coffin-makers in the streets of Singapore. February 1970

Many-templed Durbar Square, Kathmandu February 1970

Chapter 5 India

At Birganj we met our Penn drivers, one English the other Belgian, in the Automiesse coaches from Zeebrugge which were to take us all the way to the English Channel. The next morning, we crossed the border into India. As was always the way with the Indian authorities, a border crossing, especially with a large number of people could be a tedious business. One must be patient especially when dealing with India bureaucrats. Hubert and Maritza performed the task that I would be doing next time I crossed the Indian-Nepalese border almost ten years later. We passengers amused ourselves as best we could in the small border town of Raxaul. For a time a local Indian magician and his young stooge entertained us but as time went on, it was a game of marbles between a member of our group and the local boys that became the centre of attraction. With great hilarity, the game progressed until finally we got the call that all immigration and custom formalities were now complete and we could head on to Patna. The road to Patna was narrow and obstructed with slow ponderous bullock carts, donkeys, pedestrians and overloaded Tata trucks. Darkness fell well before we reached the city. This was my first taste of travelling at night in the Indian subcontinent when all daytime hazards are exacerbated by the lack of any form of street lighting, something I would become used to, but always be uncomfortable with, in the future.

The next morning, I had my introduction to the abject poverty I had always been led to believe was prevalent throughout India. We made a brief stop in the small town of Arrah in Bihar State. At the time I noted in my diary that the town must be one of the 'filthiest' in this area of India. The town was crowded with people, houses appeared in disrepair – *'tumbledown and filthy'*, were the words I used in my diary although I did say it had been raining which probably made it seem worse and *'the narrow main street was a sea of muck'*. It was here that I first encountered wandering cows, goats and pigs. This was really the first true Indian town that we had stopped in and so, I guess, made the greatest impression on my then rather naïve mind. It was here also that we first came across the crowds of impassive locals who would gather around our tour coaches and just stare. This is at first disconcerting to most Westerners but something that you just have to get used to – and accept, no matter how hard.

Later that day we visited the Sher Shah Mausoleum in Sasaram, the first example I had seen of classical Indian Moslem architecture. Built in the mid-16th century from red sandstone, this massive tomb stands in the middle of an artificial lake. Sher Shah Suri was one of the last Afghan rulers of India. He was first known as Sher Khan after he supposedly killed a tiger with his bare hands, then as Sher Shah Suri after becoming Emperor. He had seized the Moghul Empire from Hamuyun in 1540 and was succeeded on his untimely death in 1545 by his son Islam Shah Suri who died in 1554, after which the Moghul Emperor Hamuyum was able to wrest back the Empire for his son and successor, Akbar the Great. It was just on dark and had been raining, heavily, when we drove into Varanasi.

A highlight of any trip to India is a visit, in the early morning, to the bathing ghats on the River Ganges at Varanasi, known in the days of the British Raj as Benares. Varanasi is the holy city of the Hindus, the city of the great god Shiva who, adherents believe, resides here. It is here that the mighty Ganges curves in a huge sweeping bend which the Hindus have likened to the crescent moon, a symbol of the great god Shiva, and so the city has become *'the perpetual abode of Shiva and his consort Parvati: every pebble being equal to Shiva.'* If they are fortunate enough, Hindus come here to die and to have their bodies cremated on the Marnikarnika Ghat. As god of death, Shiva is also the conqueror of death. *Mrityunjaya*, the flame of eternal fire which emanates from Shiva's third eye, consumes all material bodies and Marnikarnika, the great cremation ground at Varanasi is the living symbol of this process. To be cremated here and to have ones ashes scattered in the Ganges liberates the soul from the human body, freeing it from the endless cycle of birth, death and rebirth and paving the way for union with Brahman, the absolute, the ultimate goal of all Hindus. Varanasi presents a unique combination of physical, metaphysical and supernatural elements and thus is the main focus of Hindu pilgrimage.

In the half-light of an early morning we made our way down to the ancient Dasaswamedh Ghat, already crowded with devotees performing their ablutions in the murky sacred waters of Ganga, the river – a goddess in her own right. The sun was just beginning to rise through the morning mists on the other side of the river as we boarded row-boats for what was to be an ethereal journey past the bathing and cremation ghats of this holy city. The temples and buildings of Varanasi disappeared into the misty haze as we were silently oared past the Marnikarnika Ghat. Here several bodies were being prepared for cremation and one was well ablaze, with shaven-headed male relatives in close attendance in accordance with Hindu custom. It was sobering to see this age-old ritual being performed with dignity and devotion, although the wandering mangy pi-dogs seen hanging around this ghat was rather disconcerting. Sounds, voices, chanting echoed across the waters but did not seem loud. Pigeons and crows scavenged on the shore, the odd pariah kite, or shite hawk, swooped overhead, while upon the crumbling buildings overlooking the cremation ghats vultures hunched ominously.

There were many temples on the river's bank, several having been inundated in the past by the waters of the Ganges and, with the weakening of their foundations, tilted crazily. As the sun rose higher we were back on the ghats, walking through the spice and dye markets to visit Kashi Vishwanath, the holiest temple in the city dedicated to Shiva, the destroyer. Although there has been a temple to Shiva on the site for thousands of years, the current one has only been here since 1780. The previous ancient temple had been completely destroyed on the orders of the Moghul emperor Aurangzeb, a devout Moslem, in the late 17th century. The golden spire gives the structure its common European name, the Golden Temple.

That evening, at the Hotel de Paris in Varanasi, we were treated to a concert by two of India's leading traditional musicians, Shivnath Misra on sitar and Ishwarlal Misra on tabla. Although I was aware of the sitar player Ravi Shankar through his association with the Beatles, this was my first true encounter with classical Indian music. Shivnath Misra was then an up and coming musician who later became recognised as a world-wide exponent of the sitar and became Head of the Classical Music Department of the Sanskrit University in Varanasi. Classical Indian music can be rather tedious to Western ears, but the recitations that evening were not too long, were instructive and were followed by classical dancers, Ram and Annapurna, with a traditional interpretation, through dance, of extracts from the Hindu epic, the *Ramayana*.

From Varanasi we drove on through Uttar Pradesh, India's most populated state, which had a surprising amount of open land, especially away from the Ganges Valley. Large-wheeled bullock carts were common, and we also began to encounter the sleeker camel carts. I noted in my diary that a highlight had been coming upon about fifty vultures feeding on the carcass of a dead water buffalo. This was a sight quite common in India in the '70s and '80s, but the vulture population in India declined dramatically in the 1990s and early 2000s.

Our next destination was the small town of Khajuraho in the neighbouring state of Madhya Pradesh, famous for the elaborate temples dating from the 10th to 12th centuries. While the temple complex at Khajuraho was architecturally very impressive, it was the erotic sculptures on the temples that most people came to see. Eroticism in religious art in India is common in both Hindu and Buddhist temples and has its origins in earlier tribal cults of fertility. In Hinduism the temple represents the Cosmos, *'where sky and earth embrace, and the marriage of Sky and Earth is re-enacted with the divine coupling of deities, or simply the love of ordinary mortals'* as represented in the *Mithuna* (sensuous couples amorously entwined) and *Maithuna* (couples in copulation or foreplay) sculptures decorating sections of these temples in Khajuraho. In an age when sexually explicit material was not commonplace, these sculptures were, to us in 1970, incredibly risqué. Also at Khajuraho is a complex of ancient Jain Temples. Jainism is another of the austere religions of India founded by the Mahavira, a contemporary of Siddhartha Gautama, the Buddha, in the 5th century BC. Adherents of the Jain religion, known as Jaina, believe in the complete sanctity of all life and followers are often seen wearing mouth and nose masks to avoid injuring the tiniest of insects and even the microbes in the air, and sweeping the path ahead of them, brushing aside any insects that may be there. Jain temples are particularly beautiful, with detailed decorative marble work and distinctive large-eyed sculptures of the Tirthankaras, the Jaina saints.

From Khajuraho our route took us back into Uttar Pradesh and past the fortress city of Gwalior to Agra, home of the Taj Mahal. This famous white marble sepulchre was built on the orders of the Mogul Emperor Shah Jehan in the 17th century to entomb the body of his beloved queen Mumtaz Mahal, who died, giving birth to their 14th child, in 1631. The proportions of the Taj are perfect. Everything, including the attendant buildings and gardens, are symmetrical. The main marble-domed tomb, decorated with semi-precious inlaid stones, is the ultimate celebration of love that a man can give a woman. Shah Jehan, a romantic who now rests in the tomb beside Mumtaz, was so impressed with the end result he wrote:

> *The sight of this mansion creates sorrowing sighs*
> *And the sun and the moon shed tears from their eyes*
> *In this world this edifice has been made*
> *To display thereby the creator's glory.*

The first time I saw the Taj Mahal it was raining hard and we were so disappointed. I would have to wait almost ten years before I saw it in the bright Indian sunlight. My first view, through the gate, took my breath away – even in the rain it was magnificent. I walked around the Taj in cold heavy rain, and I was to suffer in following days with a heavy cold setting in, but it was definitely worthwhile. The Taj is certainly a magnificent building, the epitome of architectural excellence and justly deserves its place as one of the Seven Wonders of the Modern World.

The nearby Red Fort of Agra is another impressive building; solidly constructed of red sandstone on the banks of the Jumna River. It was here that Shah Jehan spent his final days a prisoner, his throne having been usurped by his son Aurangzeb, the last of the great Moghul rulers. The former Emperor, now a sad and embittered man was confined to just a few rooms in the fort, but his son was not completely heartless as from his bedroom in the Red Fort Shah Jehan could gaze across the Jumna River to the fabled tomb of his beloved wife.

Just a few kilometres from Agra is the now abandoned Moghul city of Fatehpur-Sikri. Purpose-built in the 16th century by Akbar the Great who chose the spot after a Sufi saint, Salim Chishti, who lived in the vicinity, prophesied that Akbar would soon sire a son who would survive. Fatehpur-Sikri was the first planned city of the Moghuls who had established themselves in India two generations before. Shortly after the future Emperor Jahingir was born Akbar moved his court to the brand new capital. The Mogul court occupied Fatehpur-Sikri for just a short time, around 14 years, before abandoning it in favour of Lahore, for reasons that are not completely clear but are believed to relate to a lack of a reliable water supply. Much of the city remains intact. The white marble tomb of Sheikh Salim Chishti dominates the courtyard in front of the main mosque, the Jama Masjid. A palace of red sandstone, richly decorated, is intact and includes the five-storied Panch Mahal, or harem. The Diwan-i-Am, or Hall of Public Audience and the Diwan-i-Khas, or Hall of Private Audience which has a central pillar upon which Akbar sat while in consultation, also shows minimal wear and tear. It had been raining just before we visited, and puddles of water still lay in the courtyard but did not detract from the faded magnificence of this gem of Moghul architecture. As we left the massive Buland Gate, the main entrance to the city, a scrawny Indian, calling himself a diver, said he would 'dive' off the ramparts into the stagnant waters of the moat for a small monetary consideration. He received a small sum and jumped rather than dived into the murky waters. The things people do to make a living in India – and this gentleman probably made a good living by local standards!

The countryside became much drier as we approached the pink city of Jaipur in Rajasthan. Camel carts were more frequent and on many of the barren hills we could see the remnants of ancient Rajput forts. Jaipur, which I came to know very well in later years, was one of the most pleasant cities that I visited in India. Dating from 1727, Jaipur was the first planned city on the Indian sub-continent and the epithet 'the Pink City' dates from the visit of the Prince of Wales, later King Edward VII, in 1875 when the whole city was painted pink, and pink it remains to this day. The city's founder, Maharajah

Jai Singh II was also a mathematician and an astronomer and he built an amazing celestial observatory in the centre of the town. The Jantar Mantar is a collection of fourteen precision instruments, geometric devices for measuring time, predicting eclipses, tracking stars and planets, ascertaining the declination of the planets and determining celestial altitudes *etc*. The Samrat Yantra, which dominates the Observatory, is the world's largest sundial and the shadow cast by its gnomon, moving visibly at one millimeter per second, is accurate to about two seconds.

Thirteen kilometres from Jaipur is Amber, the old capital, dominated by a fort and palace. Most visitors take the cumbersome elephant ride from the village up through a gate in the outer ramparts to the parade ground before the Palace itself, an area now cluttered with souvenir sellers and a much-photographed spice and nut seller. Amber Palace has been restored to much of its former architectural splendour and is, in turn, dominated by the Jaigarh Fort which, in 1970, was not open to visitors. The Amber Palace, original home of the former ruling Kachhawa clan of Jaipur, is entered through the impressively painted Ganesh Pol, dedicated to Ganesha, the elephant-headed god of the household and perhaps the most popular deity in the Hindu pantheon. But to me the most impressive sight at Amber was the Shish Mahal, or Hall of Mirrors. Thousands of tiny mirrors stud the walls and ceiling of this airy pavilion and at night, the flickering of dozens of oil lamps give the impression of being under the starry firmament of the heavens. Over the years many mirrors have been gouged out, souvenired by uncaring visitors and although restoration work continues at a slow pace, the skill of mirror-inlay is a dying art.

It was at our hotel in Jaipur that I had my first and only experience with a fortune teller. If his predictions about my future were anything to go by, he should have been looking for a new career! While he correctly told me my mother's name, my age and my former line of work – probably through some form of trickery as I had to write these on a piece of paper supposedly hidden from his sight, his predictions about my future were way out. I was supposed to meet the lady I would marry the following August and be wed in 1971! In fact, it took a further 12 and 15 years respectively for those events to happen! As with all charlatans, to justify a failure, this fortune teller said that if I told anyone, the future he had predicted would not happen – guess I must have told someone!!

From Jaipur we headed to Delhi, the Indian capital, along a route that was then unsealed for much of the way, and with recent rains the road was exceptionally muddy. In Delhi we stayed at the Ranjit Hotel, an establishment I came to know well in future years. The 'Ratshit' Hotel, relatively close to Connaught Circus and the centre of New Delhi, was well known and used on the Overland routes well into the 1980s.

Delhi is an ancient city, believed to be the site of Indraprastha, the capital of the Pandavas, heroes of the Indian epic the *Mahabharata*, said to be the longest poem ever written. At least seven major cities have occupied the modern site, and the latest, New Delhi, was constructed by the British to the architectural vision and design of Sir Edwin Lutyens between 1911 and 1931. As Hubert and Maritza had to obtain our visas for Afghanistan and Iran while we were in Delhi, there was plenty of time for us to explore.

One of the major attractions in Delhi is the Qutb Minar, the world's largest brick minaret, which dates from 1193 and took almost 200 years to complete. It was originally built as part of the Quwwat-al-Islam, or *Might of Islam*, one of the earliest mosques in India. In the courtyard of the mosque is the famous 'rustless iron pillar' of Delhi. Believed to be over 1600 years old and of 98% pure wrought iron, this pillar is a masterpiece of the ancient metallurgists' craft. The pillar celebrates the reign of the Gupta king, Chandragupta who ruled northern India in the 4th century. I had recently read about the pillar in Erich von Daniken's first book '*Chariots of the Gods*', which had been published in 1968, one of the first books to claim extraterrestrials had visited earth, and he used the iron pillar of 'unknown alloys' as one of his 'proofs' of the presence of aliens among us. Von Daniken has long been discredited, and the exact composition of this iron column is known. In fact von Daniken admitted this in a later *Playboy* interview, flippantly saying of the Pillar: "*we can forget about this iron thing*"!

From the top of Qutb Minar I was able to look down on the Iron Pillar as visitors, prompted by the popular tradition that if you could rest your back against the pillar and make your hands meet behind it, you would have good luck. Sadly, neither of these actions are now possible. Visitors can no longer climb the stairs inside the Qutb Minar – a tragedy in 1998 in which 25 school children died led to a restriction of access, and a fence now encircles the Iron Pillar as, ironically, chemicals in human sweat had been causing the pillar to corrode.

Night life in Delhi was limited in 1970, as the region was then designated a dry State and when you were able to find a beer or a wine it was expensive. We did find the Cage Discotheque, spending an evening dancing to a local group called the 'Silencers'. One night Hubert arranged for us to attend a performance of *Kathakali* dancing. Originating in the south Indian state of Kerala, *Kathakali* is a highly stylized classical dance-drama in which the performers wear elaborate costumes and brightly coloured makeup. I recently found the programme for this performance and the synopsis makes interesting reading:

" *RUGMANGADA CHARITAM by Mandavappalli Ittirarissa Menon is a Kathakali play with great emotional and dramatic appeal. The story tells of the entanglement of good king Rugmangada with the enticing female Mohini, leading to an overwhelming tragic denoument (sic.). The enchantment of pleasurable emotions and the final climax full of terror and pity make a study in contrast."*

I do remember being rather bored through the long performance, mainly because I did not really grasp the gist of the story, but it was worth it just to see the exquisite makeup and the costumes of the actors.

Finally, it was time to leave Delhi. Visas had been obtained and we were on our way north, first through the Punjab to the city of Amritsar. We were following the famous Grand Trunk Road "*... such a river of life as nowhere else exists in the world*" which once stretched from Chittagong, now in Bangladesh, to Kabul in Afghanistan. It was along this road that Kim, the wide-eyed young traveller of Rudyard Kipling's creation, journeyed with his Tibetan lama friend. However, today no *".... long-haired, strong-scented Sansis with baskets of lizards and other unclean food on their backs"* jog-trot the road. The troops of native soldiers on leave *"rejoicing to be rid of their breeches and puttees"* no longer *"chatter their way south"* nor does the *"money-lender on his goose-rumped pony"*. But the *"Akali, wild-eyed, wild-haired"* and the *"little clumps of red and blue and pink and white and saffron, turning aside to go to their villages"* are still to be seen in ever greater numbers. En route we stopped in the small city of Ambala and it was here I saw my first leper, a woman whose nose was eaten away and most of her fingers were missing. This experience was to have a profound effect on me, something I have never forgotten.

Amritsar is the holy city of the Sikhs whose main shrine is the Hamandir Sahib or Golden Temple situated in the Pool of the Nectar of Immortality (*Amritsar*) in which is housed the *Guru Granath Sahib,* or holy scripture of the Sikhs. Built in the late 16th century the Golden Temple is one of the most striking religious buildings in India and Sikhism, founded by Guru Nanak late in the previous century, is a monotheistic religion based on the principles of faith and justice. Nanak travelled widely and studied all religions before he made the pronouncement: "*I shall follow God's path. God is neither Hindu nor Mussulman and the path which I follow is God's*". A popular story told about Nanak was that when he was in Mecca, he was found sleeping with his feet towards the Kaaba. A Moslem kazi who saw him, angrily objected. Guru Nanak replied asking the kazi to turn his feet in a direction in which God or the House of God is not. The kazi understood the meaning of what the Guru was saying - "*God is everywhere*". There were 9 Sikh Gurus before Gobind Singh, the 10th, nominated the scripture *Guru Granath Sahib* as being the 11th and last Guru.

We visited the Golden Temple in the early morning. The white marble was cold beneath our bare feet as we walked out to the Temple, staying for a time listening to the chanted readings from the holy *Granath* to the accompaniment of musicians on harmonium and tabla.

A morsel of food was offered before we walked on around the Pool of the Nectar Immortality. This was another Temple that I was to become familiar with in later years, before Indira Gandhi ordered the tragic attack, both for her personally and for the Sikhs, on the complex in 1984.

The erotic sculptures on the Temple of Khajuraho in Madhya Pradesh were regarded as rather risqué by the standards of 1970

It was raining heavily the first time I saw the Taj Mahal, but the monument was still magnificent. February 1970

Chapter 6 Pakistan, Afghanistan & Iran

In 1970 the border crossing between India and Pakistan was near Ferozepore, some distance south of the current and more direct crossing at Attari Road. This was due to the ongoing tensions between the two countries which culminated in the Bangladesh war 18 months later. After a delay of around 4 hours clearing both Indian and Pakistani immigration and customs, we drove to Lahore, the second largest city in Pakistan.

Lahore was one of the great cities of the Moghuls and like Delhi, is dominated by a Fort built by the Emperor Akbar in the 16th century. Close by is the distinctive 17th century red sandstone and white marble Badshahi Mosque, built by Emperor Aurangzeb and, for over 300 years after its completion, was said to be the world's largest mosque. I climbed a minaret from which there was a tremendous view over the old centre of this teeming city.

Outside the Lahore Museum is the 18th century cannon Zamzama, better known as 'Kim's Gun': "*He sat, in defiance of municipal orders, astride the gun Zam-Zammah on her brick platform opposite the old Ajaib-Gher - the Wonder House, as the natives call the Lahore Museum.*" I had not read Kipling's book at the time of my visit but after having travelled along the Grand Trunk Road and now seen this cannon, I knew it was just a matter of time before I did. This magnificent artillery piece was cast in Lahore by Shah Nazir, a metalsmith during the reign of the Afghan King Ahmed Shah Durrani and was one of the largest pieces of ordnance cast on the Indian sub-continent.

Our stay in Lahore coincided with the annual Lahore Horse show which was a very colourful spectacle. I, along with other group members, spent the morning feeling very much like pukka sahibs, sitting beneath a colourful canopy watching charging lance-wielding horsemen tent-pegging, show horses 'dancing' to the beat of a drum and camel-riders, not to be outdone by the horsemen, manouevring their more awkward lolloping mounts into position to also scoop out tent-pegs with their lances. It was a scene reminiscent of the days of the British Raj, from which the spectacle had its origins.

My first impressions of Pakistan on my first visit were good, writing in my diary that it seemed so much cleaner than India, the people were proud and hated India! I remember one Pakistani predicting, quite adamantly, that Pakistan and India would be at war within two years. As history shows, he was quite right as the Indo-Pakistan War over Bangladesh broke out in December 1971! As we drove out of Lahore the next morning a prison truck full of students, arrested for protesting against a visit to Pakistan by the Shah of Iran, went past us – a grim reminder, even then, of the unpopularity of the Shah.

After a very good pepper steak lunch at Rawalpindi, most welcome after the tough water buffalo 'beef' we had had in India, we crossed the Indus River at Attock by the old bridge. This bridge had originally been constructed in 1883 and was rebuilt in 1929. The upper level carried the Lahore-Peshawar railway and the lower level the Grand Trunk Road. The bridge and the approaches were heavily fortified by the Pakistani army and photography in the vicinity was strictly forbidden. There was also a very tight turn the drivers had to make to get our Automiesse coaches onto the bridge, the original designer not having envisaged modern 50-seat tour coaches using the road.

Peshawar, our next overnight stop was very much a frontier town then, as it still is now. The city, gateway to the Khyber Pass, was my first contact with the Pathans, a proud people who inhabit much of the North-West Frontier Province of Pakistan, the Khyber Pass area and a good proportion of southern Afghanistan. First impressions, when we pulled up outside the grandiloquently named Hotel International, were not good with a crowd of leering Pathan men gathering around the coach and harassing the ladies. In later years I came to know the Pathans much better and began to understand their ways, but in 1970 it was the first time I had come across the rather twisted way in which many Moslem men regarded Western women, their impressions having come mainly from a misinterpretation of male-female portrayals by Hollywood and the restrictions placed on Islamic women.

The Khyber Pass was a highlight of the Overland. It was a place of romantic adventure, one of those larger-than-life places that I had read about as a boy, and now I was there. At Jamrud, the small town regarded as the gateway to the Pass, I saw tribesmen going about their daily business, rifles slung casually over their shoulders, hanging precariously onto back access ladders or squatting uncomfortably on top of rickety local buses as they headed off into the foothills of the Hindu Kush. To me it was an unreal sight. Regimental plaques near Jamrud Fort commemorated the British and Pakistani troops who, over the past hundred years, had been stationed in the Khyber Pass. Hubert related stories of the tragedies invaders had experienced here over the centuries as we wound our way along the tortuous road, past Landi Kotal, to the border settlement at Torkham. Here there was the inevitable wait while formalities on both the Pakistani and the Afghan sides were completed, before we were allowed, rather late in the day, to proceed on to Kabul.

The route to Kabul takes the traveller through the spectacular and dangerous Kabul Gorge. The road is narrow and tortuous, but fortunately traffic was sparse along the series of terrifying switchbacks, zigzags and hairpins all with sheer drops of several hundred feet to the Kabul River far below. Failing light meant I was unable to take the photographs I wanted, and it was just after dark when we drove into Kabul.

Kabul in 1970 was still a peaceful place and an important stopover on the hippy trail to Kathmandu. The tragedy that became Afghanistan was still a number of years away. King Zahir Shah ruled the country and my first impression of the people was positive, they were friendly. Even now I find it hard to believe how the Afghanistan I first visited in 1970 could degenerate into the lawless, terror-haunted country it now is. All thanks to foreign interventions.

Kabul appeared relatively modern although I noted in my diary that the state of the roads left a lot to be desired, with no proper pavements and, after the heavy rain of the previous days, very muddy. Early March was the tail end of winter and it was cold, with snow sitting on the hills around the city. During an excursion down Chicken Street, a well-known shopping area, I purchased one of the Afghan wool-lined leather coats that were fashionable in the late '60s and '70s. I commented at the time that many of the coats had a definite 'aroma' to them, possibly because the leather was not treated as well as it could be. My coat, lined with the local karakul wool, seemed OK, but some months later it began to go mouldy in the damp London weather and I surreptitiously left it behind in a flat … somewhere! It was in Kabul that I first saw women in full burqa and I was fascinated by the turbaned tribesmen who wandered the streets. I noted in my diary that there were many soldiers and that Russian influence, even then, was very noticeable. Food in Kabul was good and I ate one night at the Khyber Restaurant, an institution in those days that every Western traveller visited and on another night, I had a turkey meal at the Spinazar Hotel which cost 60 afghanis (about 80 cents NZ). I wrote in my diary that this was the best meal I had had since I had left home - and the cheapest!!

After leaving Kabul we drove through a snow-covered landscape as we headed toward Ghazni. The day was clear but cold and a stop was made for the many Australians in the group who had never been in snow. Of course, there was the inevitable snow-ball fight! Ghazni was the former capital of an Empire, established in the 11th century by the rather vicious Mahmud of Ghazni, that once encompassed Iran, Afghanistan and much of northern India. In 1970 Ghazni was a small town with muddy streets, horse-drawn carts and disconsolate donkeys. The town was dominated by an ancient mud-brick fortress occupied by the Royal Afghan Army. We lunched at Sultan Mahmoods, a local restaurant, enjoying a local rice dish which was cheap and tasty, before heading on to Kandahar.

Kandahar is the second largest city in Afghanistan and, in recent years, has been a hotbed of Taliban activity, but in 1970 it was a rather quiet little town with not a great deal of interest. We were only there overnight and spent a good part of the evening looking for somewhere suitable to eat. We entered some wild joints, thick with hashish smoke before finally settling on the balcony of the Kandahar-Heart Gate Tourist Hotel to a shish kebab meal. Our entertainment that night was watching the antics of a lone policeman on the traffic island outside the hotel. He was on points duty and every time a car came along the street – about once every five minutes – he would spring into action, enthusiastically directing the motorist in a direction the motorist had no intention of going. He would shrug then, hands behind his back, walk around his little island until the next car came along when once again he would spring into action.

From Kandahar our route to Herat took us through the desert toward the small town of Farah. One of our coaches blew a front tyre and left the road in this barren area of desert. Fortunately, the vehicle stayed upright, and no one was hurt but it did take a couple of hours to repair the wheel and get the coach back onto the road before having a late lunch at the Farahrod Hotel, a modern-looking facility built by the Russians in the late 1960s. It appeared to have all modern facilities, but no one stayed here as, despite its modern appearance, there was no electricity, hence no heating or power for the water pumps which also meant the toilets didn't work. We were ushered through the hotel, which boasted a modern kitchen, into a grubby old shed out the back where all they could offer us were omelettes cooked on a Primus stove.

It was after dark when we arrived at the Herat Hotel, on the outskirts of the city of Herat. This was also a modern hotel built by the Russians and magnanimously gifted to the Afghan people. Electricity was also limited here with no heating and lights going out relatively early.

This hotel also had a large Olympic-size swimming pool which had never had water in it! It seems there were several similar hotels in northern Afghanistan that had been built by the Soviets, but no thought had been given to the utilities required to run a large hotel and no training had been given to the local Afghans when the hotels were handed over.

The main point of interest in Herat is the Friday Mosque (Masjid-e Jami), known for the detailed beauty of the blue tilework that completely covers the façade of this 13th century place of worship. On the outskirts of Herat is a complex of minarets known as the Gawhar Shad Musalla. These 15th century constructions are now under threat from a local major highway carrying heavy lorries to Kabul, but in 1970 all was quiet. The minarets had withstood the tests of time although the once beautiful blue tile work had been seriously damaged, although it was still picturesque.

The next day, with three companions, I headed into Herat. A sudden shower of cold, spring rain lashed the muddy streets as we four clambered into a horse-drawn *tonga*. The poor old horse's back legs lifted off the ground, so a re-distribution of weight was required before we set off. Extra *afghanis*, the local currency, were proffered to the driver to overtake any other *tonga* we came across on the road, especially if occupied by other members of our tour group, and soon the poor horse was sweating, steaming profusely in the cold Afghan air as we raced towards what excitement this frontier-like town could offer. The carriage stopped with a jolt and we jumped onto a muddy pavement wet from the recent rain. Wisps of smoke curled upwards from the wood fires in a dozen lean-to shelters, evidence of tea being brewed and meals being prepared. We ambled along the sidewalk, peering into the fuggy interiors of many small shops. Lee, a brash New Yorker, entered a little store. We followed closely behind. This shop was typical of those found throughout the East, with bric-à-brac ranging from firearms and hurricane lamps to needles, nails and brass samovars scattered carelessly throughout. The interior had the unmistakable smell of the locally treated leather of karakul sheepskin coats that hung haphazardly in every available space. We began fossicking through the merchandise while Lee approached the little Afghan storekeeper. He innocently asked if there was an *Astra* automatic pistol in stock. Yes, the Afghan replied, he has one in his safe and in a moment returned with what was seemingly an *Astra*. Lee examined the pistol closely for a minute or two, looked intently at the shopkeeper and said with a smile "*This is made in Afghanistan*." The Afghan hesitated for a moment, unsure, then replied: "*No, no, made in Spain. See! Here is mark.*" Sure enough the engraving on the pistol said it was made in Guernica, Spain. Lee smiled and pulled from his pocket his own *Astra* automatic which he had bought in Spain. He had, in the last year, travelled by motor-bike through Central and South America and had felt the need to carry some sort of protection. This little automatic would fit snugly into the confines of his toilet bag. In a day or two we would be crossing into

Northern Iran and had been warned by Hubert that baggage searches, instigated by SAVAK, the Shah of Iran's secret police, would be far more assiduous than elsewhere in Asia, and any discovery of narcotics or firearms would definitely be frowned upon, severely – we had been warned! Lee placed his automatic upon the table. "*No*" he said emphatically "*this made in Spain*." The little Afghan's hands fell to his side and his mouth dropped open. Recovering, he reluctantly admitted his pistol was locally made. We compared the two weapons and even to a dilettante like me, knowing very little about firearms, the locally-made version was obvious. Bolts and screws were larger and more roughly made, the overall finish of the weapon was not as refined and, I was told, it took a different calibre bullet. To the inexperienced or to a local purchaser who was offered this weapon it would undoubtedly be taken to be the genuine model. The Afghan now looked at Lee. "*You sell!*" "*Yes*". Lee and the Afghan sat down, tea was called for and a lengthy, entertaining haggling session began.

Crossing the border into Iran was a lengthy process – 4 hours getting out of Afghanistan and 5 hours getting into Iran, and it was quite late when we finally arrived, after a rough drive over unsealed roads, in Mashhad, then Iran's second largest city. This city is also one of the holiest in Iran, boasting the Golden-domed tomb of Imam Reza, the 8th Imam of Shia Islam. Here Hubert warned us about the 'friendly Iranian students practicing their English' saying that they could quite likely be SAVAK agents – the Shah's secret police - and to watch what we said. Sure enough, the next morning a young man, a schoolboy, approached me asking questions in English – what does 'dark horse' mean and what are the English equivalents of the mathematical signs + - x =. He was thankful for the help and walked with me for a while. I doubt very much if he was actually a SAVAK agent – but who knows!

In those days alcohol was freely available in Iran and I have noted in my diary that the local beer, Argo, cost 40-50 rials, or 55-65 cents NZ.

The drive between Mashhad and Gorgan was the longest so far on the trip, some 450 miles, much of it over unsealed corrugated roads which soon turned to mud when it began to rain. During the afternoon, our coach was forced off the road by a local truck and became stuck in thick mud. After two hours, with the help of locals and a 6-wheeler Czechoslovakian Tatra truck, we were finally extracted, the locals having tried three times to tie a knot in a length of steel towing-rope which had snapped! On the fourth attempt it held. It was after midnight when we finally reached the Miami Hotel in Gorgan.

From Gorgan it is not far to the Caspian Sea coast at Babolsar. This was our first glimpse of the World's largest inland sea and first impressions were not particularly good. The beach at Babolsar was dirty, with rather fine sand covered in debris, both organic and man-made. A little further out the water was shallow and muddy. The day was grey with a cold wind blowing inshore but a couple of hardy souls from our group, English and German I believe, decided they just had to have a dip in the Caspian Sea. We ate sturgeon kebabs at a beach restaurant before continuing along what became an increasingly attractive shoreline with local sturgeon fishing boats hauled up on the sands. At the town of Chalus the road turned inland to wind up and over the Elbruz Mountains, an area of spectacular scenery which unfortunately disappeared in the encroaching darkness. In was late evening when we finally reached Tehran.

Iran in 1970 was still well under the control of the Shah and SAVAK, the secret police. It was a rule of fear, although to visitors this was not so obvious. The unrest perpetrated by the Ayatollahs was yet to come. We only stayed one night in Tehran, as we would have to come back in a few days to extend our visas. As we drove south into the desert towards Isfahan we passed through several small towns. It was the Day of Ashura, an important day for Shia Moslems in the Islamic month of Muharram. To commemorate and to show their grief at the death of Hussein, grandson of the prophet Mohammed, and his family at the Battle of Karbala in 680 AD, processions of devout Shias perform self-flagellation using what appeared to be shiny flails made from bicycle chains. We saw several of these processions and were warned not to take photographs as the devotees would be very worked up and quite likely to turn on unbelievers on this, one of the most sacred days in the Shia calendar.

Our route took us through the town of Saveh, where Marco Polo, in the late 13th century, claimed he was shown the tombs of the Biblical Three Wise Men, the Magi: '*In Persia is the city called Saveh, from which the three Magi set out when they came to worship Jesus Christ. Here, too, they lie buried in three sepulchres of great size and beauty. Above each sepulchre is a square building with a domed roof of very fine workmanship. The one is just beside the other. Their bodies are still whole, and they have hair and beards.*' Saveh, also a centre of the ancient fire-worshipping religion of the ancient Persian prophet Zoroaster, was sacked by Tamerlane just over 100 years after Marco Polo's visit and presumably the 'sepulchres' were destroyed. During the course of the day we were able to inspect a section of the intricate *qanat* system of irrigation developed in ancient Persia. In these arid regions, horizontal waterways from a water source have been painstakingly dug at varying depths beneath the surface. Vertical access shafts break the surface every 20-40 metres. This ingenious system has provided fresh water to the desert areas without the risk of losing too much water through evaporation.

As we progressed south through the Iranian desert, a front tyre on our coach blew – and we had no spare, that had already blown out. We were therefore stuck in the desert for two or three hours while makeshift repairs were made. Close by were the remains of an abandoned desert habitation which I described in my diary: "The dwellings had been hewn out of the desert. The entrance had been reinforced with mud-bricks. Air vents were spaced down the main tunnel which had been hewn into a hemispherical shape about 5 feet 6 inches high. The whole structure must have been down to a depth of 15 feet below ground level. One tunnel had another small room adjacent to the tunnel which had evidently been used as living quarters. A stone fireplace was situated in the centre of the room under a smoke outlet." I suspect that this may have been the remains of an earlier caravanserai, now slowly crumbling under the depredations of the elements. It was after midnight when we limped into Isfahan with just three wheels on the single back axle, the other wheel having been transferred to the damaged front.

Isfahan is one of the most beautiful cities in Asia. The central feature of Isfahan is the Naqsh-e Jahan, which translates as 'Image of the World Square' but was commonly called Shah Square until 1979 when it was renamed Imam Square. It is one of the largest city squares in the world and is surrounded by buildings from the Safavid era (late 16th – early 17th century). The blue-domed Shah Mosque is situated on the south side of the square. On the west side is the Ali Qapu Palace built in the late 16th century by Shah Abbas I. The Sheikh Lotfollah Mosque is situated on the eastern side and the northern side of the square opens into the Isfahan Grand Bazaar. The Isfahan Bazaar is one of the oldest and largest in the world and was certainly fascinating to this lad from New Zealand. Brassware, carpets, kilims, jewellery in gold and silver, the famous tile work, enamelware, semi-precious stones, spices, all the treasures of the ancient East were found here. Hours could be, and were, spent wandering round this vast emporium. Outside in Shah Square horse-carriages still plied their trade but, for an amateur photographer like myself, the great Mosques with their intricate tilework were a delight.

A walk across the early 17th century Seeyosepol, or Bridge of 33 Arches, over the Zayandeh Rud, the local river, took me to the Armenian Quarter of Julfa. Here I visited one of the early Christian Churches, the Vank Cathedral, and I was fascinated by the graphic wall murals, painted in vivid colour, of the martyrdom of early Christian saints such as Boniface, John, George *etc*. Many of the murals were higher up and in semi-darkness but this somehow seemed to add to the horror of the scenes of saints being dragged over nails, beaten with sticks, flayed alive, castrated or having boiling oil poured over them; probably very effective in keeping a simple, uneducated congregation on the straight and narrow. To further remind them of the correct righteous ways, as decreed by the clergy, when they returned home, a large mural depicting the horrors of Hell had been painted immediately above the door. The Armenians, who had suffered their own diaspora, had arrived in large numbers, fleeing Ottoman persecution in the late 16th and early 17th centuries.

In 1970 there was a large American presence in Iran, mainly connected with the oil industry and in Isfahan there was the American Advisory HQ which had a social club to which we were invited for drinks and to see the new movie 'Ice Station Zebra'. When I next visited Isfahan, all had changed and Americans were *persona non grata*.

On our way south to Shiraz a stop was made at Naqsh-e Rustam, the Necropolis of the early Persian kings. These large tombs have been cut out of a bare rock-face and include those of Darius the Great, Xerxes I and Artaxerxes. One of the most interesting features of Naqsh-e Rustam is the large rock-cut relief of the Roman Emperor Valerian surrendering to the Sassanian king Shapur I after the Battle of Edessa in 259 AD.

Shiraz, city of poets, literature, wine and flowers – perhaps not of wine now that Iran is an Islamic Republic – is entered via the Koran Gate. Hafiz, one of the most famous Persian poets lived in Shiraz in the 14th century:

For a mole on the cheek of my darling,
  Which the breezes of Shiraz have fanned,
I would gladly surrender Bukhara,
  Or give back to its Khan Samarkhand.

We visited the tomb of Hafiz, situated in an attractive garden in the town, but the main reason for coming to Shiraz was its proximity to the ruins of ancient Persepolis, the once magnificent city of the Persian kings that was finally destroyed by Alexander the Great in 330BC. This was the first of the classical ruins I had visited and I was suitably impressed. Much of the restoration work in 1970 had been completed by Italian archaeologists and, in particular, the bas-reliefs on the stairs leading to the Apadana Palace, showing details from the lives of these ancient Persian kings and their subjects, were almost pristine. Remnants of some of the columns of the Hall of 100 Pillars had been restored and the remains of a horse-head capital rested regally in the ruins. The hillside tomb of Artaxerxes III afforded a great overview of the site which gives an idea of the huge extent of this ancient city. Persepolis, the name literally means 'city of Persians', dates from 515 BC and was originally built as the ceremonial capital of the Achaemenid Empire founded by Cyrus the Great. The Macedonian, Alexander the Great was an admirer of Cyrus but he finally destroyed the Empire and Persepolis in 330BC.

We returned to Tehran via Isfahan. Tehran was a city that held no charm for me. It was busy, bustling and just a jumble of the old mixed with the new. From Ferdowsy Square I could see the distant snow-capped Elburz Mountains which looked inviting. Red Soviet flags, paired with green, white and red flags of Iran decorated the Square. We heard that a senior Soviet politburo member, Nikolai Podgorny, was paying a visit to the city. We ended up staying five days in Tehran while waiting for our visa extensions. One morning group of us decided to get out of town. We hired a mini-van with driver and set off to the ski resort of Shemshak in the Elburz Mountains. From memory, the ski-slopes were mainly for experienced downhill skiers, of which I certainly wasn't one. When I asked if there was a beginners' slope I was directed to the chairlift up the mountain. My informant either misunderstood me, or had a very wicked sense of humour. Far from being the gentle slope I had expected, the slope seemed to fluctuate from the almost vertical to the vertical. I was terrified, and it took me a couple of hours to finally reach the bottom; although the experienced skiers in our group saw nothing untoward in the steepness of the slope, there was no way I was going to repeat the experience. The day ended with a delightful impromptu exhibition of Armenian dancing, however my lingering memory of Shemshak is a cluster of rather lengthy icicles hanging over the doorway of an old stone hut.

From Tehran we headed to the border with Turkey by way of Tabriz. Close to the border is the unusual town of Maku situated rather precariously in a gorge in the surrounding hills. A massive recent rockfall appeared to have devastated buildings in a section of the town. At the border post of Bazargan there was a long queue of trucks on the Iranian side and we had time to kill while Hubert and Maritza completed formalities. From Bazargan I could see the two mountains, Lesser and Greater Ararat, both old snow-covered volcanic cones. It is upon Greater Ararat that Noah's Ark, according to *Genesis 8:4,* ran aground after the Biblical flood: '*and in the seventh month, on the seventeenth day of the month, the ark came to rest upon the mountains of Ararat.*'

The muddy streets of Ghazni, Afghanistan on an early Spring day in March 1970

Horse-drawn carriage in front of Sheikh Lotfollah Mosque in the centre of Isfahan, Iran. March 1970

Chapter 7   Turkey to London

Once through the border we spent our first night in Turkey at the Kent Hotel at Doğubayazıt, or 'Doggy Biscuit' as I later came to know it. Most of us camped in the hotel grounds. It was here that occurred the first, and only, unpleasant incident of the entire journey. As was not unusual, a large number of local men gravitated towards the Kent Hotel when they knew an Overland group was in and I guess it was a combination of alcohol and the misinterpretation of the friendliness of one of the Australian girls which led to an incident which, although I did not witness it, led to a confrontation between the hotel manager and an over-amorous local. The locals were asked to leave. There may have been blows, but there was one rather upset Australian girl who had objected to what appeared to be a physical advance as she returned to her tent. The locals left, with much shouting and threatening that they would return – in force. Some stones were thrown at the tents and for a time all males of the Penn Overland group held the ground floor while the females stayed upstairs. However common sense eventually prevailed, and the threat came to nothing, although we all had a pretty uneasy night. The sequel occurred the following morning when the manager approached the lady who had been molested and asked her if she would like the offender to be publicly beaten! Evidently it had been agreed that he had been in the wrong and this was the retribution. The lady in question magnanimously declined to oversee the punishment which, of course, never went ahead, but it appeared that honour was satisfied all round.

It was a chilly morning as we drove through eastern Turkey passing several poverty-stricken Kurdish villages where the inhabitants scratched out of meagre living from the rather barren land. Erzurum was the first major town we came to and I recorded in my diary how I was not particularly impressed with the 12th century Double Minarets for which the town was renown, but I did enjoy my first döner kebab, which, along with salad, a sweet and a beer, cost just over 11 Turkish lira, or about 80c at the then exchange rate. Next morning, I looked out of the window of my room in the Polat Hotel into one of the city squares. Several local buses were warming their engines, an old van and a truck moved slowly past a number of local Turkish share-taxis whose drivers stood around chatting. These vehicles are known as a *dolmuş*, which means in Turkish, appropriately, 'seemingly stuffed'. But what caught my eye was the number of horse-drawn carriages also being prepared for the day's business.

Snow still lay thick upon the ground as we crossed Kopdağı Pass and drove to the charming small town of Bayburt once an important stop on the old Silk Route and still dominated by the remains of a large Byzantine Fortress on a rocky hill to the north of the town. Marco Polo visited Bayburt and observed that there was a large silver mine in the area. The main street leading directly to the Fortress has the ubiquitous bust of Mustapha Kemal Atatürk as its centrepiece. Just about every town in Turkey has, in pride of place, a bust or statue of the founder of the modern Turkish Republic who, incidentally, had been the nemesis of the Anzacs at Gallipoli in 1915. Between Bayburt and the coast at Trabzon we passed through the delightful little Ikisu Valley. The name means two waters, or the meeting of the waters, and the first signs of Spring were just beginning to appear. Blossoms covered many of the trees and a couple of women were tilling with hand hoes, a fertile garden plot contained within a stone wall. The tinkling waters of the Ikisu River added to the restful serenity of this isolated valley.

Trabzon is a port on the Black Sea and was once known as Trebizond, but it was the amazing Sumela Monastery that we had come to see. This Byzantine Monastery had been constructed on a narrow ridge on what, at first sight, appeared to be a sheer cliff 300 metres high in the Altındere National Park. The original Monastery dated from the 4th century and, according to legend, was built on the site of a cave where two monks found a miraculous icon of the Virgin Mary. Added to over the centuries, Sumela became an important place of Christian learning and pilgrimage until the 1920s when the monks left during the large population exchanges on the breakup of the former Ottoman Empire. Although the site had been abandoned for some 50 odd years at the time of my visit, there was still much of interest here. Byzantine frescoes still remain, many defaced by the local Moslems who do not believe the human form should be depicted in art. In the Rock Church there is a fine depiction of Jonah being swallowed by the whale along with other well-executed Biblical scenes and paintings of the Saints, Jesus and the Virgin Mary. The views from the Monastery across the valley are stunning and the toilets of the monks put a completely new meaning to the term 'long-drop'!

Cappadocia and the Göreme Valley were always favourite stops on the Overland routes. This fascinating area was overlaid by volcanic tufa blasted out by a large ancient eruption, about 10-11000 years ago, of the stratovolcano Erciyas Dağı and over the millennia wind, rain and ice have sculptured the region into a dramatic moonscape of pinnacles and rills modified by the hand of man. Churches, dwellings, workshops, even entire cities have been cut into this soft volcanic rock. The whole area is a photographers' delight. We stayed in the small town of Ürgüp surrounded by the delightfully named Fairy Chimneys. These are eroded tufa formations capped by chunks of harder volcanic rock. The fascinating history of human habitation in the area goes back to the early persecutions during the nascent years of Christianity, and perhaps even earlier, but it was from the 4th century that much of the underground work began. Some of the first churches date from the early iconoclastic period of the Byzantine church in the 8th century, when it was decreed that human form should not be depicted in church art. Fortunately this period did not last long and there are some magnificent frescoes in some of the later churches of Göreme. Over the centuries many of the frescoes have been damaged, particularly after the big decrease in the Christian population of Turkey after World War One. Eyes and faces on many of these works of art have been scratched out, but in the Dark Church, so called because of the lack of windows, most of the paintings are intact. A guide indignantly told us that a more recent case of vandalism occurred during the filming of the opera *Medea* in the 1960s with the famous diva Maria Callas. According to our informant, the film crew, on instructions from the director, modified one or two of these troglodytic dwellings causing irreparable damage so they could obtain a better photographic angle, or was it to make things easier for Maria Callas?

One of the most fascinating features of the Göreme region is the underground city of Kaymaklı. I had never heard of this place prior to my visit and found the place absolutely fascinating. No one really knows how far back in time this subterranean city goes, but it is supposedly connected by an 8 km tunnel to the equally expansive Derinkuyu underground complex. Kaymaklı was built over at least seven levels and was capable of supporting two to three thousand people. Perhaps it dates as far back as the Phrygians (5th century BC) but it was certainly expanded considerably in Byzantine times by various waves of mainly Christian refugees. This complex is truly mind-blowing. There are many other underground complexes in Cappadocia, but Kaymaklı and Derinkuyu are the best known and the largest. Passageways are narrow with little head-room and most of the rooms small, although there are larger common rooms, kitchens, storerooms and churches. This confusing labyrinth of interlocking rooms and corridors is certainly claustrophobic, and the thread of Ariadne would certainly be a necessity if one ever became lost here. Kaymaklı is ventilated by large hand-dug airshafts, seemingly bottomless. The local guide lit a sheet of newspaper and dropped it into a shaft, letting it spiral down into black oblivion below.

In Ankara we visited Anıtkabir, the Mausoleum of Mustapha Kemal Atatürk, which is situated on a hill overlooking the city. Regarded as the Father of Modern Turkey, Atatürk had been the Turkish commander on the Gallipoli Peninsula, successfully organising the defence against the Anzac forces in 1915. While not throwing the invading forces back into the sea *per se*, he was able to contain any advance by the Anzac, British and French forces until they eventually abandoned the Peninsula by early 1916. He then served with success against the Russians on the Eastern front in the Caucasus. After the collapse of the Ottoman Empire, Atatürk organised the Turks during the Turkish War of Independence. The Ottoman Empire had rather foolishly been divided, by the Treaty of Sèvres in 1920, between Greece, Armenia, France and Britain with a relatively small area of Anatolia bordering the Black Sea being left in Turkish hands. The Treaty, which was signed by Ottoman representatives, was not recognised by Atatürk and, making his headquarters in Ankara, he organised the Turkish forces into a very effective army. After defeating the Armenians in the South Caucasus and the French in Cilicia, the Turkish forces finally defeated the Greeks at the Battle of Sakarya in 1921. The Treaty of Lausanne, ratified by Atatürk in 1923, established Turkey's borders as they remain today, and Constantinople, now renamed Istanbul, remained in Turkish hands as did the crucial straits of the Dardanelles. During the War there had been atrocities perpetrated by both sides culminating in a massacre of Greek and Armenian citizens in Smyrna, now Izmir, and the burning of the city. This was followed by a large-scale population exchange between Turkey and Greece and even today there is still ill-feeling between the two countries.

Ankara was now the new capital of the Turkish Republic and Mustafa Kemal became the 1st President. He then embarked on a programme of modernisation. He decreed that Turkey would now be a secular state switching the weekly 'day of rest' from the traditional Islamic Friday to Sunday, bringing it in line with Europe. He brought a number of women into his parliament, something unheard of during the Ottoman era, he banned the wearing of the fez, Latinised the Turkish alphabet and introduced the requirement that all men should have surnames. He adopted the name Atatürk, which means the 'father of the Turks' and it is forbidden by an act of the Turkish parliament for anyone else to use that surname. Atatürk ruled with an iron fist and a French journalist once wrote that Turkey was governed by one drunkard, one deaf man and three hundred deaf-mutes. When he heard this, Atatürk is said to have commented, *'This man is mistaken. Turkey is governed by one drunkard.'* He died in 1938 and the large mausoleum on Anıtkabir was constructed between 1944 and 1953. This large, rather sombre, edifice is approached by a triumphal alley flanked with neo-Hittite lions. The halls surrounding the mausoleum also doubles as a museum dedicated to the life of Atatürk and the War of Independence. After seeing the changing of the goose-stepping Military guards of honour at the Mausoleum we headed off across Anatolia to Istanbul.

In 1970 the bridges that now span the Bosporus had not been constructed, although preliminary work on the first bridge had begun just a month or so earlier. We had to cross by ferry from Üsküdar, formerly known as Scutari. We could see the minarets and domes of the Sultan Ahmet (Blue Mosque), Sulimaniye Mosque and Aya Sofia, the former Byzantine Cathedral, silhouetted against the late afternoon sky as the ferry steamed past the lighthouse known as Kizkalesı, or the Maiden's Castle and around Seraglio Point and into the Golden Horn. We were staying at the BP Mocamp, the main camping ground on the outskirts of Istanbul and a place I was to get to know well as a tour leader ten years later. The camp has now disappeared under the urban sprawl of rapidly growing Istanbul.

Istanbul is a fascinating city, a true melting pot of both European and Asian cultures. Greek, Roman, Byzantine and Ottoman ruins and buildings intermingle to give the city a character found nowhere else. Legends and stories of intrigue, tragedy and heroism abound here more than in any other European city, for that is what Istanbul is, a European city which was, in fact, the last capital of the Roman Empire. To me the most significant building here is Aya Sofia, originally the Greek Orthodox Cathedral of the Holy Wisdom. Now over 1500 years old, Aya Sofia had, for over a thousand of those years, the world's largest dome – until the construction of St Peter's Basilica in Rome in the 16th century. After the capture of Constantinople by the Ottoman Turks in 1453, the Cathedral became a mosque and after Kemal Atatürk became President of modern Turkey, it became a Museum which, appropriately, it remains to this day. I have visited Aya Sofia several times over the years and have always had a true feeling of history as I walk around the massive granite, marble and porphyry columns, beneath the dome, semi-domes, pendentives and arches, richly decorated with a mélange of Byzantine mosaics and Islamic calligraphy, and around the large marble lustration urns from Pergamon. I am always intrigued by the depressions on the stone steps at the Imperial Entrance which I was once told was the result of centuries of wear by the Varangian Guards, the Viking mercenaries who once served the Byzantine Emperor. I find it incredible that this magnificent building has been here pretty well unchanged for longer than *homo sapiens* have lived in my native New Zealand. Nowadays the Sultan Ahmet, or Blue Mosque, with its 6 minarets is probably better known and has become one of the icons of Istanbul, and while impressive, it was built over 1000 years after Aya Sofia.

The Blue Mosque is also a beautiful building, constructed in the early 17th century and getting its common English name from the exquisite blue tiles that line the interior giving the whole building a sense of bluishness. The domes and semi-domes, supported by massive columns, are awe-inspiring. This is also one of the few mosques to have six minarets. When the mosque was built, six was the same number of minarets as the Mosque of the Kaaba in Mecca and the Ottoman sultan came under criticism from the Moslem leaders, so, as Mecca was also part of the Ottoman Empire, he ordered another minaret to be added to the Mosque in Mecca, thus preserving the architectural purity of the newly constructed Blue Mosque. From Sultan Ahmet I walked with some friends to the famous Lale Restaurant, better known as the Pudding Shop. The Pudding Shop was then the major meeting place in Istanbul at the beginning, or end, (depending on which direction you were travelling) of the hippie trail to Kathmandu. Here travellers could swap stories and information or leave messages on a notice board requesting, or offering, rides, or just posting notes of a personal nature. The interior was thick with tobacco smoke and I could smell the distinct odour of more than one joint! I had one of Lale's famous fruit puddings before we walked around the corner to the Yerebatan or Basilica Cistern, a multi-columned water reservoir dating from the time of the Byzantine Emperor Justinian in the sixth century. The Cistern had featured in the 1963 James Bond movie, *From Russia with Love*.

Before leaving Istanbul, I visited the famous Topkapı Museum, the former Palace and seraglio of the Ottoman sultans. Topkapı is situated on Seraglio Point and looks directly across the Bosporus to the Selimiye Barracks at Üsküdar where Florence Nightingale treated the wounded of the Crimean War. It also dominates the entrance to the famous inlet known as the Golden Horn. I spent some hours here wandering around the many pavilions, courtyards and kiosks. In the Imperial Treasury, I was flabbergasted by opulence of the jewels such as the 86 carat Spoonmakers Diamond, an uncut emerald the 'size of a brick', a coffee cup decorated with over 300 emeralds and the bejewelled Topkapı dagger, the subject of a 1964 movie, starring Melina Mercouri (later the Greek Minister of Culture), Peter Ustinov and Robert Morley, which was about a heist of this famous dagger. In another section there was what was, reputedly, the right hand of St John the Baptist (the hand with which he baptised Jesus), encased in a brass reliquary with a small opening revealing the bone and the dried remains of sinews. This macabre exhibit dates back to a time when it was fashionable throughout Christendom to collect holy relics of the Saints, pieces of the 'True Cross' or 'nails' used in the crucifixion. On this first visit I did not have time to visit the famous Harem of the Ottoman Sultans.

From Istanbul we travelled through Thrace to the northern Greek coastal towns of Alexandroupolis, Kavalla and Thessaloniki for a first taste of true European culture and cuisine. In Kavalla, I experienced my first

Mediterranean meal – *kalamari* – which I had never had before and commented in my diary that it was delicious, and I was amazed when I saw, for the first time, a stall selling live snails in the Kavalla market. I had always thought that this was a peculiarly French thing! Greece in 1970 was under the régime of the Colonels, the military junta which had seized power in 1967 and forced King Constantine II into exile. Banners and posters of the 'Revolution' showing a phoenix rising from the ashes, guarded by a soldier, were everywhere.

We stopped briefly at the ruins of Philippi where, after the murder of Julius Caesar, the armies of Brutus and Cassius were defeated in 42BC, by those of Mark Antony and Octavius, who later became Augustus Caesar. That night we camped on a beach within the shadow of Mt Olympus, home to the Greek gods of old. With the advent of Spring, trees were blossoming, their rich pink flowers contrasting with the daisy and buttercup-speckled green pastures. A ruined shepherds' hut set the scene and, in my imagination,, I could see goat-legged satyrs chasing lithe nymphs through these Arcadian fields. As if to confirm that the gods still do inhabit Olympus, flashes of lightning lit up the mountain that night. As I commented in my diary at the time: "*At first I thought it was the result of Constantino's Greek wine, but other people also saw it* (the lightning)."

The next day we stopped in the Tempe Valley at a small bubbling spring where, according to legend the unfortunate nymph Daphne was changed into a laurel tree by her river-god father Peneus to escape the amorous advances of the god Apollo. While I had known some of these stories from the classical myths, it was the association with specific sites that gave these stories real meaning. In later years other sites would be brought into my commentaries as a tour leader; the River Meander in Aegean Turkey where the unfortunate nymph Echo, having been spurned by narcissistic Narcissus faded away to ... an echo; the site near Delphi where Hercules (Herakles) wounded the Cerynean hind before capturing it; the Bosporus, the cow's crossing, where the nymph Io, seduced by Zeus and changed into a heifer by a jealous Hera, was pursued by a gadfly, crossed to Asia and later became the Egyptian goddess Isis. I loved these stories and to associate certain places with these and many more myths was one of the satisfying aspects of being a tour leader.

Spectacularly situated on the slopes of Mount Parnassus, Delphi is another of these ancient sites wrapped up in myth and history. As the site of the famous oracle of the god Apollo, many important prophecies instrumental in the history of the ancient world originated here. The answers the supplicants received could be ambiguous, for example, when the Lydian king Croesus consulted the Pythia as to whether he should wage war on the Persian king Cyrus, he was told: If Croesus crosses the river Aly, he will destroy a great kingdom. He crossed the river and the kingdom destroyed was his own! A more famous prophecy that had far-reaching consequences occurring during the Second Persian War in 480BC. The Persian army under Xerxes I was sweeping all before it and looked set to conquer all of Greece. The Greeks consulted the Delphic oracle and were told that: 'a wall of wood alone shall be uncaptured.' Thermistocles, a Greek leader, interpreted this as telling the Greeks to take to their ships and in the ensuing Battle of Salamis, the large Persian navy was decisively defeated by the much small, feistier Greek navy. The ambiguity of these prophecies is best illustrated in the answer given to an anonymous young Greek who asked if it would be safe to join a military campaign. His answer was 'Go, return not die in war.' It obviously makes a big difference if a comma is placed before, or after, 'not'.

The centre of Delphi was the Omphalos, the centre of the world, once guarded by the earth-dragon Python who was killed by Apollo. It was at the Omphalos that the priestess, the Pythia, possibly heady on gas emissions from a chasm beneath the temple, pronounced her prophecies. Today the ruins are impressive, with the remains of many treasuries, temples, a theatre and a stadium bearing evidence of the richness and importance of Delphi in Classical times. The acoustics in the theatre were amazing. I sat on a step near the top of the theatre and could hear Hubert, who was standing in the orchestra, quite clearly relating the history of this amazing place.

Athens was a city that more than lived up to its expectations. To be able to wander around this ancient city, to climb over the Acropolis - and in those days there was free access to the interior of the Parthenon - in the absence of crowds was a bonus in itself. Five of the original six Caryatids (female figures) were then still *in situ* on the Erechtheum; they were removed to the Acropolis Museum in 1979 and those now exposed to the elements are copies. While scrambling around the ruins of the Acropolis, I met an older American who had visited Little Barrier Island off Auckland some years before and knew Rodger Blanshard. Very few New Zealanders have stayed on Little Barrier and to meet, here in the ruins of the Acropolis in Athens, an American who had stayed with the same person I had in New Zealand seemed an amazing coincidence. The ruins of the great Temple of Olympian Zeus were deserted the morning I walked around it and as it was early in the tourist season there were few people watching the changing of the Greek guards outside the then Royal Palace, even though the king was no longer in residence.

Next morning, I walked, with an Australian friend, to the 11th century Byzantine Monastery at Dafni. The church here has some exceptionally fine mosaics, most particularly that of Christ Pantocrator which covers the entire dome, and again we were the only visitors.

On the way to the Greek border with Yugoslavia we stopped at Thermopylae. It was here at the pass that Leonidas and his 300 Spartans held up the Persian army led by Xerxes during their advance on Athens in 480 BC, an event that led to the afore mentioned Battle of Salamis. In those days the sea was much closer to the mountains than it is today. It was also here in 1941 that the ANZACs fought a delaying action against German tanks during the invasion of Greece. At the time of my visit red poppies spattered the fields around Thermopylae. While I called them 'Anzac' poppies in my diary, the Greek symbolism was the same – they are said to have sprung from the drops of blood from Leonidas and his men. There is a large statue of Leonidas at Thermopylae with the inscription: '*O stranger, go and tell the Lacedemonians that we lie here after obeying their commands.*'

Yugoslavia in 1970 was firmly in the grip of Josip Tito and the break-up of that State was still many years away. We stopped in the small town of Niş where we visited the macabre Cela Kula, or Skull Tower. This symbol of nationalism made a deep impression on me as I had not seen, or even heard of, such a sinister monument before. It was only during later travels that I learned that such skull towers where not uncommon during the depredations of Genghis Khan and, particularly, Tamerlane. This particular tower had been built, with the skulls of Serbian patriots killed by the Ottoman Turks during an uprising in 1809, as a deterrent against any further opposition to Ottoman rule. I reached out and touched one of the yellowing skulls that still remained in the original mortar as a mark of respect to these patriots of long ago.

We made a stop at the Postojna Caves, now in Slovenia. This is one of the largest cave systems in

Europe and we travelled some 2 kilometres by electric train deep into the cave. There are some very fine stalactites, stalagmites, speleothems and other cave formations, particularly in an area known as 'Paradise'. Interesting inhabitants of the Postojna Caves are what the locals called 'human fish'. These are, in fact, olms or white salamander - *Proteus anguinus* to use their Latin name. These unusual creatures are blind and the skin has lost much of its pigment due to their chthonic existence, which gives them the appearance of having 'human flesh'. They were first seen in the 17th century when heavy rain washed a number of olms out of the caves. The locals believed them to be the offspring of a cave dragon. During the Second World War the occupying Germans had used a section of the caves for the storage of aviation fuel and in 1944 Slovene partisans blew up the dump causing a fire that burned for a week and destroyed a large section of the caves. The first hundred metres or so was still blackened from this event.

Our last major stop on the Overland was in Venice. It was early Spring, temperatures were cool and the crowds of Summer had not yet arrived. To me, and of course to the others of the group, it was a novelty to travel to and from the Youth Hostel on Giudecca Island, by *vaporetto*, or water bus. Just after we arrived, much to my surprise, a Panamanian registered ship, the *New Zealand Venture*, steamed slowly past towards the shipping terminal. I can't say I knew it from home!

Venice is a fascinating city, in complete contrast to the hustle and bustle of all the other cities we had visited. The lack of traffic noise was its most outstanding feature. Although we travelled between islands by *vaporetto*, Venice is a great city for walking with many narrow lanes running between ancient piazzas and along and over the numerous small canals. While in Venice I did all the touristy things – saw the Bridge of Sighs and the Doge's Palace, visited the Basilica of St Mark, sat in a café in St Mark's Square amid the pigeons sipping an overpriced coffee, walked over the Rialto Bridge and along the Grand Canal and visited a Murano glass factory. It was my first real taste of Renaissance Europe and I liked it. I wrote in my diary at the time that "*the whole place is just fantastic. After Kathmandu I think it is, perhaps, the most exciting city I have been to.*" Venice was not normally on the Overland route and this was the only time I visited the city while on a London to Kathmandu journey. On all my later journeys, in the late '70s and early '80s, I travelled straight to Athens through Germany, Austria and Yugoslavia.

From Venice we drove over the Brenner Pass and into Austria, stopping in grey, rainy Innsbruck for a couple of nights. I noted in my diary that the beer and the wiener schnitzel were good. After a night in Heidelberg we followed the Rhine through West Germany and into Belgium where we stopped a night in Brussels. We stayed in the Hotel Duc de Brabant and I remember remarking to one of my companions at the time that I would not like to be in the warren-like corridors of the hotel if it ever caught fire. Seven years later this hotel did catch fire and 19 people perished. From Ostende we crossed the English Channel on the Belgian Marine ferry *Roi Leopold III* and when I saw the White Cliffs of Dover appear through the murky haze of the English Channel, I knew my first Overland journey had well and truly come to an end.

The amazing tufa formations of Cappadocia in central Turkey were little visited in 1970

In 1970 the first Bosporus Bridge had not been constructed and all crossing from Asia were by ferry.

Chapter 8 Britain & France

With a couple of friends from the Overland, I spent my first night in London at a small bed and breakfast hotel in Ebury Street in Victoria. It was 30 shillings per night or, if we stayed a week, £7. We decided to stay a week which gave us time to sightsee in London and to orientate ourselves. We walked endless miles through the streets of this fascinating city visiting all the most important tourist sites. Speakers Corner in Hyde Park, in particular, fascinated me. Here there were a wealth of interesting characters spouting forth their political and/or religious messages along with the amusing interjections of hecklers. It led to an entertaining Sunday afternoon. There were Maoist speakers and other left-wing agitators; Zionists and pro-Palestinians, Black and Civil rights advocates; Catholic women preaching against the evils of birth control and on the periphery, there was always the 'Prophet of Doom' who carried a large banner pronouncing 'The End is at Hand'. But perhaps the most entertaining of the speakers was the notorious tattooed man, South African-born Jacobus van Dyn then over 70, who during the course of his entertaining performance would say how he had once worked for Al Capone and had, consequently, been imprisoned in Sing Sing. He then stripped to the waist – quickly, he said, in case the police saw him – to show his tattoos. He really was most entertaining in these days before large-scale body tattooing became common.

After a week or so reality set in and I had to get a job. My first job was through an agency as a postal messenger for a sugar business in Tooley Street, just south of the River Thames. I had to hand deliver letters and documents around the city and I can remember once my boss saying to make sure a certain letter, containing a cheque, got to the right person – it was a cheque for a £1,000,000 which was a lot of money in 1970! I had moved into a flat in Arundel Gardens in Notting Hill with others from the Overland and here I stayed for about six weeks. The flat had one interesting feature, the dining table was in an alcove that was actually situated underneath the pavement and we could hear people walking over us when we were eating – a novelty to all the New Zealanders, Australians and Americans who stayed here.

It wasn't long, however, before I decided to head out of London and took on a seasonal job picking potatoes in North Wales. This would be my first experience of rural Britain. I travelled north by bus, stopping first in Chester where I stayed with a friend with whom I had worked at Air New Zealand. He and his wife had returned to England shortly after I had left on my Overland. I spent a pleasant weekend being shown the sights of the attractive town of Chester, with a highlight being a visit to a special airshow at Hawarden Airfield where, for the first time, I saw a World War Two Hawker Hurricane and a De Havilland Mosquito in the air. On the Monday I continued my journey by double-decker into North Wales and as the bus proceeded through

Prestatyn, Rhyl to Llandudno I became fascinated by the 'unpronounceability' of the small Welsh village names, noting in my diary that 'the one that stands out is Ffynnongroew'. It was a hot day and as the heater on the bus could not be shut off, we had to change to another vehicle near Llandudno. Another bus change in Caernarfon gave me time to visit the castle where, less than a year earlier, Prince Charles had been invested as the 21st Prince of Wales. Eventually my bus left for Pwllheli where there was one final change to a local bus that took me to Aberdaron on the Lleyn Peninsula. This was the heart of Welsh-speaking, Nationalist Wales and I thought it rather bizarre to be in a bus in the United Kingdom and not be able to understand a word that fellow passengers were saying.

I was given a lift by a local storekeeper from the small, pleasant village of Aberdaron out to Carreg Farm, about two miles away and close to Porth Oer, or Whistling Sands Beach, famous for its 'squeaking' sand. Carreg farm was then owned by Michael Solari and his New Zealand wife whose name I can't now remember. Here I met my fellow pickers, from New Zealand, Australia and Canada. The work, while not difficult, was hard on the back, but we were young and knew it was just for a few weeks. We were also working with a group of gypsies from Portmadoc. They were a hard bunch, very coarse, and Mike Solari told me that one of the gypsy men had said to him that he wasn't sending his kids to school but bringing them up on the land because *'they don't teach them anything useful at school!'* One day when I was loading bags of potatoes onto the farm trailer, one of the girls yelled out: *"Come here and I'll give you a thrill."* This interchange somewhat shocked me at the time. Another morning I heard one of the gypsy girls who appeared to be very young and was obviously very worked up, yelling to another about how she would *"… kill the fucking bitch as she was screwing her man!!"*

We spent much of our down time on Whistling Sands Beach, to which there was a pleasant walk over a small hill called Mynydd Carreg on which there was a small stone wall and ruin, probably an old cattle-shelter. Bob, one of the New Zealanders who had a wicked sense of humour, nicknamed it the castle of the 'medieval warlord, Roderick the Nasty. Bob wove the tale so well that one of the Australian pickers believed him!

The town of Aberdaron with its two pubs was about 40 minutes' walk. One Saturday morning we were in town waiting for the pub to open. It was during the lead up to the 1970 British General Election when the Labour incumbent, Harold Wilson, was trying to fight off a challenge by the Conservative leader Edward Heath. I was sitting with Bob on the parapet of the small stone bridge in the village waiting for the pub to open at 11, when the local Labour candidate pulled up and got out of his car with a megaphone and began his electioneering. Within about two minutes a young man, obviously a supporter of Plaid Cymru, the Welsh Nationalist party, came out of the Ship Hotel with two saucepans and began clashing them together, drowning out the Labour candidate. When the candidate stopped speaking the clanging stopped, when he started to speak again, the clashing of the saucepans began again. It was quite a comical situation which only ended when the Labour candidate gave up in disgust, got into his car and drove out of town. It didn't have any effect on the election result, however, Plaid Cymru had no members elected to Parliament that year, and the local Labour candidate was elected, although the Conservative (Tory) Party received an overall majority and Edward Heath became Prime Minister.

From North Wales I headed down to the small town of Storrington in West Sussex, along with Bob. We had obtained work assisting with the grain harvest on Sullington Manor Farm, a place I was to know well over the next three years. I had never worked on a farm before, but it seemed that if you were a New Zealander, so the theory went, you must be a farmer. This was a great learning experience for me and one that I enjoyed. Sullington Manor Farm was an old property, having first been recorded in the Domesday Book. There was a church dating from Saxon times on the farm and the Manor House itself dated from around 1350. There was a large tithe barn, one of the largest and oldest in the south of England, on the property. It was believed that this structure dated from at least the 15th or 16th centuries, maybe earlier, and there was a date of 1685 on one of the beams which was said to be when the roof had last been rebuilt. During my stay, John Kittle, the owner had a new grain drier installed and we had to cut through one of the ancient oak beams supporting the roof. First appearance showed this beam to be rotten and eaten away by insects, but when we reached the core, it was like trying to cut through a piece of iron.

The farm was situated on the South Downs within sight of Chanctonbury Ring, an Iron Age fort dating from around the 5th century BC. There were ancient flint workings on the property and the Southdown Way, a walking track, passed through the farm. For someone like me, from the other side of the world, Sullington Manor Farm fired my imagination with the romanticism of the Anglo-Saxons, the Normans and even the earlier Neolithic settlers who must have walked these lands. Sometimes as I worked in the fields or in the garden I would be transported back to a dream world of serfs and yeomen, knights and squires which was engendered by the effigy of a knight in the old Manor church. I was to work at Sullington Manor Farm off and on for the next three years.

Albert, the head farm worker, was a character in his own right. A cantankerous old sod at times, he also had a heart of gold. If we did something wrong he would let us know in no uncertain terms, but was never upset for long. He had the interesting turn of phrase of the bucolic and was not averse to blaspheme considerably. His interpretation of events could be rather amusing. For instance, one morning he began a conversation thus:
"I see that ol' kiddie made it."
"Who's that, Albert?"

"You know, whaddayacall!" With blank quizzical expressions, Bob and I looked at each other then back at Albert.

"Who?"

"God suck me Christ (his favourite phrase), you know. Whaddayacall! Sailed round the World backwards or somethin'!"

It turned out Albert was referring to the round-the-world yachtsman Chay Blyth who had just become the first person to circumnavigate the globe sailing west to east rather than following the normal east to west route.

Another of Albert's frustrating colloquialisms was the over use of the term 'whatsisname', although this was also shared to a lesser extent by Bill, the other permanent farm labourer. Albert would use the word as a noun: "Albert, where's the hammer?" "Aw, it's in the whatsisname." Or as a verb: "Albert, where's Bill?" "Oh, he's whatsisname." One day I overheard a conversation between Albert and Bill: "Bill, get the spanners from the whatsisname." "Oh, you mean the whatsisname?" "'that's what I bloody said, in the whatsisname!"

Life working with Albert was never dull, and he often over indulged at the Storrington British Legion and Comrades Club before jumping into his green Austin A-40 and somehow finding his way home. Another time I was invited to a meal of roast pheasant cooked by Aggie, Albert's long-suffering wife. I took one mouth of the meat and couldn't eat anymore. To me it was rotten, while Albert was declaring it to be 'bootiful, just bootiful! Just how it should be!" Turned out it had been hanging for some time, as one does with pheasant. For my taste buds, it had been hanging far too long – I don't think I have eaten pheasant since! So it was with great sadness when I received a letter from Aggie when I was in South Africa several months after leaving Storrington, telling me that Albert has passed away following a massive heart attack.

Much of the recreational life in Storrington revolved around the British Legion and Comrades Club of which we were all members. There was cheap beer, and good weekend meals, darts and pool plus a band most Saturday nights. The Club Darts team competed in a local league and, while Bob and I were there, they won the regional championship in Worthing, on what turned out to be a rather good night – I think! Another time there was an excursion to Alexandra Palace (Ally-Pally) to attend the All England Darts Championship where, to copious bottles of beer, we watched at a distance, the national competitors, although large screens around the hall brought the action closer to view. It was an interesting experience. One day the Club announced that the cost of beer was to be increased – from 10p a pint to 10½p. You would have thought the world was about to end. Many of the locals said they would leave the club and drink at the local pubs – where it was 14p a pint! It was the principle, they said. I don't think any of the regulars did leave, or if they did, not for very long. While I was in Storrington, a Chinese restaurant opened in the village. It proved to be popular, but I remember a sign outside the restaurant which was headed – How to Eat

Chinese Food. The last line, in bold letters, stated: 'You do NOT order chips with Chinese food!'

From Storrington one of my first sight-seeing excursions, with Bill, the farm labourer, and his wife Vi with whom I was staying, was to Stonehenge. In 1970 visitors could walk within the Circle, under the Trilithons, and sit on the fallen stones to have photos taken or even picnic within the shadow of the stones. It was some years later that, due to increased visitor numbers, restrictions were brought into force and now this amazing and speculative site can only be viewed from a distance. Other excursions from Storrington included Petworth House, Longleat Safari Park and the beaches at Brighton and Bognor Regis which, after the beaches I was used to at home, I did not think were particularly inspiring.

I rather liked the tranquillity of Sullington and often on a summer's evening I would sit beneath the ancient yew trees in the churchyard of St Mary's, the old Manor church which dated from Saxon times, listening to the bucolic sounds of the countryside; the distant lowing of cattle, the cough of a cock pheasant in the growing wheat fields; the joyful songs of blackbirds and song thrushes and, as darkness encroached, the pinging of a bat or the distant call of an early rising owl and, if I was lucky, the melodious song of the elusive nightingale. It must have been an evening like this that Thomas Gray sat in the churchyard at Stoke Poges in Buckinghamshire in 1750 and composed his *Elegy Written in a Country*

Churchyard. I could not help feeling that the first three verses could have almost been written about Sullington.

> *The curfew tolls the knell of parting day,*
> *The lowing herd wind slowly o'er the lea,*
> *The ploughman homeward plods his weary way,*
> *And leaves the world to darkness and to me.*
>
> *Now fades the glimmering landscape on the sight,*
> *And all the air a solemn stillness holds,*
> *Save where the beetle wheels his droning flight,*
> *And drowsy tinklings lull the distant folds;*
>
> *Save that from yonder ivy-mantled tower*
> *The moping owl does to the moon complain*
> *Of such, as wandering near her secret bower,*
> *Molest her ancient solitary reign.*

From Sussex I moved on to Kent for the hop harvest near the small village of Horsmonden, not far from Goudhurst. Here I met up with some of the people I had been potato-picking with. We worked in an oast house, spreading out the freshly picked hops to dry in the kilns, before bagging them for shipment to a brewery. In the evening, we could walk to the local pub or watch television in our accommodation, and it was here that we all saw *Monty Python's Flying Circus* for the first time. This was an immediate favourite and the morning after one episode saw the entire group of pickers 'silly-walking' to their respective posts!

During September 1970, the major international news story was the hijacking and eventual destruction of four passenger jets and the subsequent hostage drama that was played out at Dawson's Field near Amman in Jordan. The destruction of three of the planes, shown on TV, after the hostages had been released brought home, for the first time, the real threat terrorists from the Middle East could pose. Jordan then descended into a brief but bloody civil war between the Jordanian army and factions of the Palestine Liberation Organisation, the culmination of which saw the ouster of the PLO from their Jordanian bases and the untimely death of President Nasser of Egypt the day after he had brokered a cease-fire between the warring factions. I was to get to know Amman and Jordan well in later years.

By late September the hops had been gathered and a group of us travelled across to France for the grape-harvest. This time we crossed the English Channel by hovercraft, which I noted was quick but relatively uninteresting, and caught the train from Boulogne to Paris. The next day, after a morning sightseeing in Notre Dame, where I climbed up to one of Quasimodo's bell towers, we caught an afternoon train to Tours, transferring to a 'packed' railcar to Saumur in the Loire Valley. At the station, we were picked up by Carol de Tigny and taken to the Domaine Vinicole de Chaintre of few kilometres out of town where we would work during the *vendange*, or grape-harvest. This was always an enjoyable experience and one I repeated in 1971 and again in 1972.

Chateau de Chaintre which dated from the 17th century was owned by Gael de Tigny and his American wife Carol. The vineyard of about 50 acres was a classic example of a *clos*, meaning it was completely enclosed by a stone wall. The work was quite hard, particularly on the back, if you were clipping the bunches of grapes off the vine. Some of us, mainly the males, would have large plastic panniers strapped on our backs into which the pickers would empty their buckets. When the panniers were full we would walk to the trailers, placed in the area that was being picked, climb up and empty our panniers into the large wooden vats on the trailer. They would then be taken to the winery. We had a lot of fun picking, and the interaction with the local villagers in a combination of both broken French and English led to much hilarity. My schoolboy French was a little different from the local patois of this region of France. Meals during the vintage, although basic, were very good and during the lunch break there would often be an 'international' game of *boulle*, now more popularly known as pétanque, in the gravelly courtyard outside. The 1970 vintage was a good one and I will always remember the grape wars that went on, especially when we picked the over-ripe, botrytis-infected, white grapes to be used for making desert wine. Splattered with sticky grape juice we returned happy from the vineyard at day's end.

During our time off we explored the nearby villages of Chaintre, Varrains and Dampierre-sur-Loire as well as Saumur and its castle. The Castle had appeared in *Les Très Riches Heures du Duc de Berry*, a French Gothic book of prayers created by the Limbourg Brothers in the early 15th century. The Castle is identifiable from the medieval manuscript where it featured for the month of September. Chaintre is just a small village with narrow walled streets around the Chateau. The larger village of Varrains had a small shop, café and a boulangerie where we would often walk for a coffee, a beer, a glass of wine, or to buy one of the very good pastries. Dampierre-sur-Loire, as the name suggests, is on the Loire River, and has a pretty little church and an extensive cave system of wine cellars. The walk to Dampierre, and to Saumur, was through some very beautiful countryside. One evening, on the night of a full moon, I walked alone a little distance from the vineyard following a narrow, darkened track. I found a small haystack which I clambered onto and sat for a while enjoying the evening. I wrote in my diary: '*The moonlight showed up the eerie details of trees, the limestone track, the vines and in the distance I could hear Rob playing his harmonica in the fields. It was a beautiful night with bats pinging around and in the old village of Chaintre I almost expected to see a 'loupgarou' (*werewolf) *lolloping along.*'

I left Saumur in the company of Rob, an American, who had also been grape-picking. We caught a train to Tours then, with the intention of hitch-hiking to Chartres, we headed out of town. We only made it as far as the tiny village of Monnaie, about 15 kilometres from Tours and it was beginning to get dark. We tried to get accommodation in a small hotel, but the lady-proprietor took one look at us, two bearded foreigners, and decided she was full for the night. Undaunted, we had a meal at a little establishment with the unlikely French name of Chez Betty, then headed out of town, eventually creeping into a haybarn to sleep. We spent a relatively comfortable night then, just as it was getting light, there was a rustling in the hay beneath us and a figure emerged and without a word headed out the door with his backpack. Rob and I looked at each other then began laughing. We had been virtually sleeping on top of the stranger most of the night without knowing of his presence. The next morning, after trying to no avail to hitch hike out of Monnaie, we decided to take a train to Paris where we split up, with Rob going off with some fellow Americans who were heading to Barcelona.

I spent several days exploring Paris and while walking to Notre Dame, I noticed a large Gendarme presence in the streets around the Palais de Justice. Student leaders of the 1968 riots were on trial and being of a curious nature I decided to walk by and have a look. It wasn't long before I was walking past rows of visor-clad stern-looking riot police with shields and batons. As I was young, had a beard and longish hair I was soon stopped and asked for '*papiers*'. After satisfying the gendarmes that I was not a threat to France or world peace, I hurriedly beat a retreat from the environs of the Palais de Justice and headed to the much safer refuge of the Louvre. I could not help thinking of the first few lines of D.H. Lawrence's poem *The Revolutionary* which I had just recently read:

Look at them standing there in authority
The pale-faces
As if it could have any effect any more.

Pale-faced authority
Caryatids
Pillars of white bronze standing rigid, lest the skies fall.

Back in London, it was now time to get a job for the Winter. Seasonal farm work was finished until at least April. I managed to obtain work as a warehouseman at an injection plastics factory on a corner of the Edgware and the North Circular Roads at Cricklewood. I was staying in a flat above a shop in Edgware with friends from the Overland and was able to get to work easily by bus. Ilsen, the founder and owner of the Company which specialised in plastic Wedgwood-style pots and planters, was a very hard man to work for. Most of the machine operators were West Indian or Pakistani and worked a twelve-hour day with just a 30-minute break around one o'clock. They would be dismissed on the flimsiest of pretexts. As one of two warehousemen, my hours were a little shorter and I did not have such a boring routine but still I had to be careful. On clocking in each morning, we were allowed two minutes' grace or would be deducted 15 minutes pay, which was pretty basic even for that time. In 1971, there was no statutory holiday on New Year's Day and we were expected to turn up for work as usual. Terry, the one-armed head storeman, who liked his beer – usually to excess, did not turn up on

New Year's Day 1971 and was summarily dismissed. Ilsen, in a magnanimous gesture, approached me and said I would take Terry's place and he would give me a pay increase of 3d (1½p) an hour, which meant my hourly rate rose from 6/6d (32½p) to 6/9d (34p) per hour! Decimal currency was introduced in Britain in the middle of the following month.

While I was at Ilsens, a couple of interesting characters passed through. One, a truck driver, began, from the day he arrived, agitating for Union representation. Ilsen got wind of what he was up to and he was gone within a week. Another guy who arrived as a storeman had served in the French Foreign Legion, joining towards the end of the Algerian War of Independence in 1962. He was a little man and kept photographs in his wallet of dead Algerians the Legionnaires had killed during the conflict, which I thought rather macabre. He did not stay long, not turning up one day and I heard that he had re-joined the Legion.

Come Spring and I left Ilsens, heading once more to Storrington to work for a couple of months before taking an organised tour to Scandinavia, the Soviet Union and Eastern and Central Europe with Kiwi Bob and Rick, an Australian who had been on the Overland and with whom I had flatted in Edgware.

The stone church of St Mary's of Sullington in Sussex, dating from Saxon time

Gael de Tigny & family outside Chateau de Chaintre, Saumur
October 1970

Chapter 9   Journey to the U.S.S.R.

The tour to the Soviet Union was operated by Sundowners with whom I was to begin work as a tour leader in 1979. We left London on the 8th of June 1971 in two coaches, one of them quite small, and this time crossed the English Channel by ferry from Dover to Zeebrugge. Our route to Scandinavia took us through Amsterdam where I first saw the extensive red-light area with the 'ladies of the night' displaying their *'wares in red-fringed window parlours, many ready to offer more than a school boy peep-show in a private cabin.'* In Copenhagen we visited the sculpture of Hans Christian Andersen's Little Mermaid, perched on her rock in the city's harbour, but I was far more interested in the Museum of Danish Resistance in World War Two. Outside the Museum was an improvised armoured car built surreptitiously by railway shop workers for use against Danish Nazis. As we crossed the Øresund waterway between Denmark and Sweden, our ferry passed close to Kronberg Castle, the 'Elsinore' of Shakespeare's *Hamlet*.

We spent a day in Stockholm, visiting the Town Hall where the Nobel prizes are awarded each year and the *Vasa* Museum. The *Vasa* was a 64-gun warship of the Swedish navy which foundered and sank on her maiden voyage in 1628. After 333 years on the sea floor, the ship was raised in 1961 and housed in a special temporary shelter known as *Wasavarvet* or the *Vasa*

Shipyard where it was being sprayed with a preserving solution of polyethylene glycol. At the time of my visit, viewing the remains of this interesting ship was limited due to the spraying but we could get some idea as to what this 17th century warship must have looked like. Artefacts of the everyday life of a Swedish sailor of that period that had been recovered from the wreck were on display in the museum.

We crossed the Baltic between Stockholm and Turku in Finland during the period commonly known as the 'White Nights', where it didn't really get dark even though the sun dipped below the horizon at around 9.30 and reappeared at 3 the next morning. The weather was flat calm and it was a beautiful morning as the boat steamed into Turku. We spent a day in Helsinki, before driving to the Finnish border with the Soviet Union which we passed through without too long a delay.

The Soviet Union was to me an eye-opener in many respects. This was my first experience of a true authoritarian Communist regime. The Soviet Union was then under the strict leadership of Leonid Brezhnev, Aleksei Kosygin and their politburo henchmen. Far from being the 'Workers Paradise' of Socialist propaganda, I was immediately struck by the shabbiness of the U.S.S.R. from the time we arrived in Vyborg, our first Soviet city. Vyborg had been the Finnish city of Viipuri until it was captured by the Russians during the Second World War, and now it certainly lacked the modernism and vitality that we had seen in Finland. I noted in my diary at the time that I was *"quite astounded at the shabbiness of the houses... and we all agreed they could use a coat of paint."* In Vyborg I had a mug of what appeared to be beer being sold by a surly woman on a street corner. It was horrid. I found out later that this was *kvass,* a fermented drink made from Russian black, or rye, bread. It is undoubtedly an acquired taste!

Not all the Soviet Union we saw was shabby. I was impressed with St Petersburg which was then still known as Leningrad; it reverted to St Petersburg in 1991. We walked across the Winter Palace Square in front of the famous Palace of the Tsars. This impressive square had been the site of the tragic 'Bloody Sunday' massacre in 1905 when unarmed demonstrators were fired upon by the Imperial Guard. Striking workers and their families had naïvely gathered in the Winter Palace Square to present a petition to their 'Little Father', Tsar Nicholas II. The resulting massacre provoked the failed Revolution of 1905, but the seeds had been sown for the Bolshevik Revolution 12 years later. The massacre had been graphically recreated in the David Lean movie *Doctor Zhivago* which had been released about five years earlier. When someone commented about how good the book by then-exiled Boris Pasternak was, our Intourist guide just dismissed it with a "Russia has many very good authors!"

The richness of the artworks in the Hermitage, formerly the Winter Palace of the Tsars was amazing, although there appeared to be no order in how these were displayed, and our Intourist guides tended to hurry us through – they had to keep to a strict schedule.

On our second morning we travelled by one of the hydroplane ferries to the Summer Palace of Peter the Great at Petrodvorets, or Peterhof. The restoration of the Palace and gardens after its near complete destruction by the Germans during the 'Great Patriotic War', as World War Two is known, was particularly impressive. It did seem ironical that such a totalitarian Soviet regime had spent the time and money to resurrect Peterhof, a symbol of the excesses of Tsarist era, but as our Intourist guide quite rightly pointed out, like it or not, it was all part of Russia's national heritage.

An important symbol of the Soviet Union's revolutionary history, the cruiser *Aurora*, was moored in the River Neva. The *Aurora*, launched in 1900, had had a chequered career and was involved in the Dogger Bank Incident of 1904 when the Russian Baltic fleet, heading to Far Eastern Russia during the Russo-Japanese War, fired on a group of British fishing boats, believing them to be Japanese torpedo boats – even though they would have been over 32,000 kms from Japan! This incident sparked a serious diplomatic spat with Britain that very nearly led to war. The *Aurora* was caught in cross-fire from the Russian fleet and suffered some damage. In 1905 the *Aurora* was one of the few Russian ships to survive the Battle of Tsushima and after seeking sanctuary in the Philippines was interned by the USA until the end of the war. On the cruiser's return to

St. Petersburg, the *Aurora* served as a training ship until 1917. Then, at 9.45 p.m. on 25 October a blank shot was fired from her forecastle gun signalling the start of the assault on the Winter Palace and the beginning of the October Bolshevik Revolution. I had first come across the *Aurora* on a postage stamp from Poland during my days as a philatelist in the '60s, so it was a thrill for me to see this famous ship. Unfortunately, we did not go on board.

We travelled to Moscow via the historical city of Novgorod, now known as Veliky Novgorod. This city had fared badly during Second World War and our Intourist guide told us that just 30 people had greeted the liberating Red Army in 1944 and that out of over 2500 stone buildings, less than 40 remained standing. We visited the large bronze monument known as the 'Millennium of Russia', in the Novgorod Kremlin before spending the night at the camping ground near the Volkhov River. I noted in my diary that: *'The camping ground here is shocking. The toilets are worse than anything in India, and the mosquitoes are there by the thousands. The water from the taps is brown and leaves a horrible scum when boiled!'*

While Moscow, particularly the area around Red Square, has much of interest, it was the visit to the Mausoleum of Vladimir Lenin that left the greatest impression on me. I quote directly from a description I wrote shortly after this visit: *'At last, slowly, the long queue began to shuffle across the cobblestones of Red*

Square. We had waited patiently for over an hour and now we were approaching the tomb of the Soviet Christ, Vladimir Lenin. The tomb is situated about halfway along the Kremlin wall in Red Square and is a simple structure of red granite. Finally, we shuffled past the armed guards and entered the cold silent edifice. As we descended, in pairs, the granite stairs, the atmosphere became colder and gloomier and at last we entered another room in the centre of which was the tomb and there lay the glass-encased, embalmed body of Lenin, lying in state as he has done since his death in 1924. The only lights in the room are directed onto the revolutionary's face and hands which give off an eerie and almost serene sheen. The only sound is the continuous shuffle of the crowd as they slowly move around the room before filing out the opposite door. In the gloom stand four machinegun-armed guards one at each corner of the glass case. On the public walkway police keep the crowd moving. Up another flight of stairs, we leave the tomb and come out into the warm Moscow summer, and now we must move along a tree-lined walk along the Kremlin wall where other prominent Russians are buried. Here lies Marshal Zhukov and there, Marshal Timoshenko (Heroes of the Great Patriotic War), here lies Joseph Stalin, dismissed simply as "General party secretary for many years" and here are the spacemen Yuri Gagarin, killed in a plane crash in 1968, and Vladimir Komarov, killed when his Soyuz 1 space capsule crashed on re-entry in 1967. At last we come to the end of 'Remembrance Row' and walk out once again onto the cobblestones of Red Square.'

I rather liked the environs of Red Square. There were the massive walls of the Kremlin and opposite the architecturally interesting GUM, or State Department store. At one end of the Square were the psychedelic onion domes of St Basil's Cathedral, then a museum, and at the other end the State Historical Museum. As I walked across the cobbles the late afternoon sun seemed to exacerbate the redness of Red Square.

When we visited the rather grand Exhibition of Economic Achievements, I was particularly interested in the Space Hall. Here were models of the various Soviet space craft including the very first earth satellite, Sputnik 1, and various capsules of the Luna programme of the 1960s, but what we all wanted to see was the first Soviet moon buggy which had landed successfully on the moon the previous year. Such robotic vehicles were still a novelty in 1971 and this 8-wheeled Russian 'dalek' didn't disappoint.

From Moscow we headed to the city of Orel where we attended an enjoyable evening of folk dancing hosted by students from the grand-sounding Orel State Pedagogical Institute. This was followed by an interesting evening of discussions. The students had obviously been specially picked as good Communist Party cadres, as much of the very one-sided conversations were about the oppressed workers of the West and how the Revolution must be exported. On the subject of international travel, it was pointed out that Soviet citizens did not need to travel as they were happy with their life in the 'Workers Paradise', unlike us people in the West who were always seeking something! The next day as we drove south out of Orel I was struck by what seemed, after coming from New Zealand, a basic and somewhat backward rural infrastructure, highlighted by a group of peasants – for want of a better word - carrying milk churns in a horse-drawn, very solidly built four-wheeled wagon, a sight I did not really expect to see in a modern nation.

The tour now took us deep into the Ukraine, then still part of the Soviet Union, and we were one of the first Western tour groups to be allowed to visit Kharkov – even our Intourist guide had not been there before. Much of Kharkov had been destroyed during the German invasion and occupation in the Second World War. In 1971 the city seemed a grey, cheerless place with the large central Square named after the notorious Felix Dzerzhinsky, founder of the CHEKA - the Soviet secret police and forerunner of the more modern KGB. We watched as local tour groups of Russians had their photos taken beneath the large statue of Vladimir Lenin that dominated the Square. Kharkov also has an interesting monument to the 19th century Ukrainian nationalist poet and artist Taras Shevchenko:

When I am dead, bury me
In my beloved Ukraine,
My tomb upon a grave mound high
Amid the spreading plain,
So that the fields, the boundless steppes,

The Dnieper's plunging shore
My eyes could see, my ears could hear
The mighty river roar.

The base of his statue is elaborately decorated with characters from his poems which reflect contemporary life in the Ukraine in the early 19th century.

Kiev, capital of the Ukraine was a much more pleasant place with a fascinating history. Overlooking the Dneipr River is a large statue of St. Vladimir, the Viking founder of Kievan Rus way back in the 10th century. Like Kharkov, much of central Kiev had been destroyed during the War, although the Perchersky Monastery seemed to have survived relatively intact. This was the first time I had been into a true Catacomb, replete with the bodies of the Orthodox Bishops who had passed on. It was rather bizarre to walk among the embalmed, enshrouded bodies, some with bony hands still covered in dried skin protruding from their funeral shrouds.

The cult of Lenin was still alive and well in the Soviet Union at this time and I remember marvelling at a huge portrait of Lenin which covered five stories of the Moscow Hotel on Kreschatik, the main street in Kiev. This street had been deliberately destroyed during the Second World War – the Russians say by the Germans, the Germans say by the Russians. Whatever the truth, most of the buildings had been destroyed and many lives were lost. What was indisputable was the fact that the Germans had a killing field outside the city at a place called Babi-yar where many Jews, and others, were summarily executed. One night at the camping ground in Kiev I had my first, and last, experience of excessive local vodka consumption and even today the thought of it turns my stomach!

We journeyed on to Odessa on the Black Sea, and walked down the Potemkin Steps which provide access to the port. During the short-lived Revolution of 1905, the Tsar's soldiers massacred many civilians on these steps during the uprising which had begun with a mutiny on board the battleship *Potemkin*. While we were in Odessa, a rather tearful Russian approached us in the street and told us that three cosmonauts, Georgy Dobrovolsky, Vladislav Volkov and Viktor Patsayev, of the Soyuz 11 space mission had died when their space capsule de-pressurised as they were returning to earth. This had been the only manned mission to board Salyut 1, the world's first space station.

Our last stop in the Soviet Union was at Kishinev, now capital of the modern state of Moldova, and it was raining heavily when we drove into this rather drab city and it was still raining the next day as we drove through the muddy streets of the border town of Leusheny where, after a slow process, we cleared Immigration and Customs, said farewell to the USSR and crossed into Romania.

It was late afternoon when we finally completed Romanian formalities and drove on into a darkening countryside which still bore evidence of the heavy rain the area had been experiencing over the last few days. It some places water was over the road. We were heading to the Black Sea resort of Mamaia, a suburb of Constanța. As we progressed through Romania we needed to refuel, but all the service stations were closed and eventually, a few kilometres short of our destination, at close to midnight, we ran out of diesel and spent the rest of the night trying to sleep in the parked bus. Early the next morning Graham, our driver, managed to scrounge a few litres which got us into Mamaia and after checking into the camping ground, we spent the rest of the day enjoying the nearby Black Sea beach. In 1971 Mamaia was still a developing resort with many hotels under construction as part Nicolae Ceaușescu's modernisation programmes. Although the day was sunny, there was a stiff breeze blowing in from the Black Sea. I went for a swim here, my first in the sea since leaving New Zealand, and commented that the water was cold. I also noted that *'you couldn't go very far (waist-deep) as life guards in boats stop you!'*

We spent an evening in Bucharest, which didn't exactly impress me, and as we were camping at a place called Snagov, around 25 kilometres out of the town, the time we were able to spend in the Romanian capital was limited.

Our continuing journey through Romania was somewhat marred when the bus I was in slammed into the back of a slow-moving lorry in the rain near the small

Transylvanian village of Vişeu de Jos, not too far from the city of Cluj. No one was injured as Graham, our driver, had time to warn us all to brace ourselves as the bus began sliding. The bus suffered a punctured radiator and a broken half windscreen. We carried a temporary plastic screen and while Graham made make-shift repairs to the radiator, fortunately the rain had stopped, we were able to explore this little village. A local lad, practising English, was only too pleased to show me and Rick through the village church. He was particularly proud of the wall frescoes of the Saints which had just been re-painted. We eventually reached the Cluj camping ground quite late after a slow journey. Several of us, sitting in the front stairwell, took turns to siphon water from a plastic jerrycan, by way of a tube, into the radiator. Graham would give us the word when he noticed that the engine temperature was starting to creep up.

After further repairs, although we still had to feed water into the radiator, we headed on through Transylvania, stopping at a small local market where the main form of transport were horse-drawn, four-wheeled wagons. Wagons were still arriving and on one sat a woman, firmly clasping a squirming, squealing piglet. This area of Romania has some productive farmland on which stooks of newly cut grain, drying in the sun, awaited collection. We cleared the border into Hungary without much delay although it was getting late when we reached Budapest. Here the radiator on our coach was finally repaired.

We had a day to wander around Budapest, an attractive city on the Danube. I crossed the river two or three times during the day and was impressed with the Parliament Buildings on the river bank which had the Red Star of the Communist regime in a prominent place at the top of the dome. I visited St Stephen's Cathedral and the old citadel which had been used by Soviet troops during the Hungarian Uprising in 1956 before catching a train back to our camping ground. Next day we had a reasonably long drive to Vienna and after crossing into Austria, the change between East and West was very noticeable. 1971 was the height of the Cold War and Soviet power in Eastern Europe was at its peak. I enjoyed Vienna, wandering around the Palaces, churches and museums of the central city before spending time in Stadtpark, lying under the trees in the sun, listening to a selection of Strauss waltzes being played by an orchestra. Our stay in Vienna culminated in a visit to the village of Grinzing to sample, probably too much, the local wines.

We drove on to Prague, then the capital of Czechoslovakia. It was only three years since the Prague Spring when the liberal reforms of Alexander Dubcek had so incensed the Soviets, but little evidence now remained of the Warsaw Pact Invasion which had created headlines around the World. Although Prague was firmly under Communist control, it did appear more vibrant than the other Eastern bloc cities we had visited. Unfortunately, we only had a day to enjoy Prague but we made the most of it, visiting all the major sites and enjoying the excellent dark beer. Prague was a great city to walk around. I photographed some interesting buildings in the area around Wenceslas Square and found the late Gothic architecture of the Týn Church with its multi-steepled towers interesting. In the afternoon I walked up to Hradčany Castle where I visited St Vitus Cathedral and the Military Museum before walking back to the city along Golden Lane, a very attractive street of small coloured houses dating from the 16th century. I sat enjoying a very beautiful sunset, reflected in the waters of the Vltava River, before walking back to our campsite.

Our journey back to London was via Cologne, dominated by the twin spires of one of the largest Cathedrals in Europe. The old city centre had been completely destroyed by Allied bombing during World War 2 but the Cathedral, although hit many times, did not collapse, the spires of which were used as a landmark by the bombers, so it was said. A few years later when I was leading an Overland tour from Kathmandu to London I had an older Canadian who was travelling with his daughter. When we reached Cologne on the last days of the tour he said to me that he had been looking forward to visiting Cologne as the last time he had seen the spires of Cologne Cathedral had been as a tail-gunner in a Lancaster bomber when the towers had been wreathed in smoke and flames. The old centre of Cologne had, of course, been completely rebuilt and the spires still dominated the city. The beautiful Belgian canal city of Bruges was our last stop before we crossed the English Channel from Zeebrugge.

In the summer of 1971 I returned to Sullington Manor Farm to once again work the grain harvest and then headed back to Saumur in France to pick grapes. This time I had plans to head on south to Spain and Morocco with the idea of working the winter in Gibraltar were I rather misguidedly thought there would be plenty of work as the border between this tiny British colony and Spain had been closed for some years.

There were familiar faces and new at Domaine Vinicole de Chaintre in 1971 and once again the harvest was a good one. After the vendange had finished, most of the other pickers drifted off but I stayed on to see the colourful vendange mass which was held in the garden of Chateau de Chaintre. The local children first paraded through the village of Chaintre: '*Preceded first by little boys in white robes, carrying a crucifix and a statuette of St. Vincent, patron saint of vineyards. Little girls in colourful costumes followed, (*and they were*) followed by Gigi's horse, bedecked in flowers, carrying two side baskets of grapes. Then came two boys carrying a miniature wine press followed by the village band playing* Marching through Georgia *and* Swanee.' To this rather incongruous choice of music, the procession wended its way through the arched gate into the garden of Chateau de Chaintre where an informal mass was celebrated by the local priest, after which the congregation was given a glass of the local *rosé d'Anjou.*

From Saumur I headed south by train, first to Toulouse then on to the ancient walled city of Carcassonne with which I became totally enamoured. *La Cité*, situated on a hill overlooking the River Aude, is dramatic and to me it evoked scenes from the Age of Chivalry, of knights and maidens, of sieges and medieval battles. It was a magical place, made even more so by the fact that the Youth Hostel was within the walls of *La Cité*. I stayed three days and there was something thrilling about passing through the Narbonne Gate with its massive towers, especially after dark, and it wasn't hard to imagine a massive portcullis isolating the city at night. In 1971 not so many people visited Carcassonne and there was hardly anyone staying in the old city at night. I spent my days exploring the ramparts and narrow streets of the old city and dining in the lower newer city. There is an interesting apocryphal story about the origin of the city's name. In the 8th century the city was then ruled by a Saracen king Baalak and his wife Dame Carcas. The city had been besieged by Charlemagne for five years and Balaak was killed. Dame Carcas, now in charge and realising that the city was on the verge of starvation, had the last pig stuffed full of what grain could be found and thrown from the highest tower. The unfortunate pig burst on impact and Charlemagne, believing the city still had plenty of food, raised the siege. To celebrate Dame Carcas ordered trumpets to be blown to summon Charlemagne and his men to parley. Hearing the trumpets, one of Charlemagne's men is said to have exclaimed '*Carcas sonne*' which means 'Carcas sounds'. At the subsequent meeting it was said that Charlemagne was so impressed with Dame Carcas's courage and guile that he allowed her to continue ruling over the city. There is, of course, no evidence that this really happened but it does make a good story!

I caught a bus from Carcassonne to the small town of Ax les Thermes in the Pyrénées. I was heading up to Andorra and had heard that this little town had a thermal pool and I decided to check it out. The Bassin des Ladres, or Pool of the Lepers, is in the centre of town and, although sulphurous, I was disappointed as it was barely warm, unlike the thermal pools I knew at Rotorua, back in New Zealand. I stayed a night here at a hotel and that evening spent 9 francs on a meal that consisted of soup, a plate of small crabs in gravy, local sausage with potatoes, a blancmange desert and wine.

It was a pleasant drive through the changing autumn leaves of the foothills of the Pyrénées to the Principality of Andorra, a tiny European country dating from the 13th century whose co-princes are currently the French President and the Bishop of Urgell in Catalonia. I spent a night in the capital, Andorra la Vella, and that evening spent 8 francs on a meal that consisted of soup, snails in garlic butter, chicken and wine. It was the first time I had eaten snails and I noted in my diary that they 'were pretty good'. My conservative New Zealand tastes were obviously changing! The next day I was offered a ride with a couple of Americans who were travelling in a

Volkswagen Kombi to Barcelona and were only too pleased to have extra company on the drive. It was late afternoon when we arrived in Barcelona and I checked into a Pension just off La Rambla, the tree-lined main street of Barcelona.

I spent five days exploring Barcelona. I had particularly wanted to visit the Picasso Museum to get a better understanding of the art of the famous Spaniard. The Museum has many of Picasso's paintings from his early – pre-1900 – and 'Blue' periods and it gave me quite a different appreciation of his artistic talents. I was particularly fascinated by his drawing simply called 'The Madman' dated 1904. The twisted visage and hands of his subject, clad in tattered rags, is to me a mark of his genius. I also spent time in the Museum of Modern Art which has contemporary paintings from Catalan, and other Spanish artists. While in Barcelona I visited the construction site of 'La Sagrada Familia', the great Church of the Holy Family designed by the eccentric architect Antoni Gaudi. The project started in 1882 and occupied Gaudi until his death in 1926. In 1971 four of the spires were, more or less, completed but very little of the nave. Work has since progressed at a much faster rate in recent decades and the church was consecrated by Pope Benedict XVI in 2010 and the projected completion date in now 2026, the centenary of Gaudi's death.

My main objective while in Barcelona was to see a bullfight and one Sunday afternoon I went along to the

Plaza des Toros. It was a colourful pageant but was something I found quite distasteful. The machismo shown by the matador, obviously playing up to the ladies in the crowd, fighting what was undoubtedly a weakened bull after the picadors and the banderilleros had done their work, culminated in the matador finishing off an exhausted young bull with his sword. It made Hemingway's comment in his book on bull-fighting, *Death in the Afternoon*: "*Killing cleanly and in a way which gives you aesthetic pleasure and pride has always been one of the greatest enjoyments of a part of the human race*" – impossible to agree with. I found nothing aesthetically pleasing in the entire spectacle.

I caught the overnight ship *Las Palmas de Gran Canarias* from Barcelona to Palma de Mallorca. In the early 1970s the Balearic island of Majorca was becoming increasingly popular with the British package holiday market. I felt I had to see Majorca for myself and must admit I was pleasantly surprised. The main town of Palma was colourful and interesting, especially away from the haunts of the holidaymakers. I ventured as far as Ca'n Pastilla where I first tried to find accommodation, but after seeing a sign stating 'We serve English baked beans' at a local cantina, decided I would rather spend my time in the old town. I spent a happy couple of days in the late autumn sun wandering around the harbour and the precincts of the Cathedral of Santa Maria, known locally as *La Seu*, and up to Bellver Castle overlooking the town. This interesting construction, dating from the

14th century, is in a good state of preservation and was the first circular castle built in Europe.

From Majorca, I decided to return to the mainland by ship to Valencia, but after finding the boat was full, I took a 3rd class berth on the overnight ferry to Alicante and caught buses, via Murcia, to Granada as I wanted to visit the Alhambra before crossing to Morocco. As we passed an airfield near Murcia, I saw, to my surprise, several Junkers 55 aircraft. These were the three-engined transport aircraft used by the Germans in World War 2.

It was raining and cold in Granada, but I was very impressed with the Alhambra palace, built by the Arab rulers of the Kingdom of Granada, which dates from the 10th century. I spent some hours exploring this masterpiece of Andalusian Islamic architecture before wandering back to the Capilla Real, or Royal mausoleum, where several Spanish monarchs are interred. One of the 'treasures' of the Mausoleum is the very gory, carved 'decapitated head' of St John the Baptist lying on a silver platter.

I was still planning to try to find work in Gibraltar, so took a bus south to Malaga. To reach Gibraltar in those days, one could not cross directly from Spain. Due to political tensions between Franco's Spain and the British over sovereignty of 'the Rock', the direct border crossing was closed and the only access was by air either directly from England or from Tangier. I therefore crossed the

Straits of Gibraltar by ferry from Algeciras to Ceuta in Spanish Morocco. Ceuta is a small Spanish exclave and fishing port on mainland Africa, surrounded on its landward side by Morocco. It is just a few kilometres to the actual border with Morocco. There were a few minor hassles at the border with a couple of Canadians I had met and who were giving me a ride. They had to have their hair cut before they were allowed entry into Morocco! We spent the night in a small pension in Tetouan and that evening, after a fish meal we ended up in a small teashop where, besides mint tea, the *keef* or hashish pipe did the rounds.

I travelled with the Canadians to Tangier and we checked into a small, somewhat seedy hotel in the central city. The small single room I was allocated was next to a rather unsavoury, shared toilet and there was a hole in the wall between my room and this odoriferous cubicle. I was not happy, so I asked the proprietor if he had another room. He said he had one other, but the key was missing. He demanded sharply that his wife bring a huge key ring and proceeded to try all the keys in the lock – none worked. We could see he was getting agitated and he sharply snapped something in Arabic to his wife who disappeared, returning a few minutes lately with a hammer. He then proceeded to attack the lock, hitting and prying to no avail. We, standing around, could see the funny side but the poor proprietor definitely couldn't. The longer the door resisted, the more agitated he became and the funnier the whole scenario. Eventually he swung the hammer back to use all his brute force against the door and the head of the hammer flew off, almost hitting one of the spectators. By now there were roars of laughter as he replaced the head. This time after couple of sharp strikes the door flew open, followed by a globule of spit, expectorated by the exasperated proprietor, to the cheers of all around. I was told I could have the room, but of course it could not now be locked. I had the choice of either an unlockable room, or one reeking of unsavoury toilet odours. I chose the former and left my backpack in the Canadians' room while we went out for a meal and smoked a bit more *keef,* coming back later well stoned. Next day, feeling a little rough, I flew with Gibair, to Gibraltar.

Collective farmer workers with a 4-wheeled milk cart near Orel, U.S.S.R. June 1971

Giant portrait of Lenin of the Moscow Hotel, Kiev. June 1971

Chapter 10   U.K. Days

Gibraltar was a disappointment. It was quite expensive and there wasn't the work available that I had been told to expect. Labouring jobs paid just £10.50 for a 6-day week. I had a bad cold, was feeling pretty miserable and after three or four days of aimless wandering, I decided to cut my losses and use some of the last of my funds to fly back to UK. I headed back down to Storrington and ended up finding work as a mill hand through the winter at nearby Thakeham. I was boarding with John and Vi in the farm labourers house on Sullington Manor Farm.

On Boxing Day there was always a peasant shoot on the farm for members of a local syndicate who each contributed a sum of money for John Kittle, the farmer, to raise a large number of pheasant chicks each year. These birds would be released onto the farm when they had matured. While not a hunter myself, I willingly offered my services as a beater, for a small amount of pay. It was always an interesting day, and not without a certain element of risk. Some of these hunters would shoot at anything that moved and during the day a rabbit, flushed by the dogs, ran towards me. Immediately one of the hunters raised his shotgun in my direction. Fortunately, he saw me in his gun-sights and lowered the shotgun, but I saw my life flash before me. During the day one of the other hunters was struck on his cheek by a wayward pellet which drew blood. Other than a good bag of pheasants, the day's haul also included ducks, partridges, several rabbits and hares, a fox and a woodcock.

1972 dawned and on New Year's Day I listed my tentative plans for the year in my diary. This was the first time I seriously considered returning to New Zealand by way of Africa. I also expressed concern about: "... *the restlessness I know I shall have difficulty in controlling that makes me dread the day I return to New Zealand with the object of settling down. Perhaps I never shall – who knows?*" I ended by quoting a paragraph from a letter sent to me from a friend from the 1970 Overland. He had written:

> 'Well, I escaped from the 'rat-race for twelve months, did a 'skit' around the world, came back to Australia, and neatly slipped back into the same old rut which I left – SHIT!!'

During the first few months of the year, I seemed to be suffering from a touch of both melancholia and nostalgia, if my diary is anything to go by. I was working as a millhand at a factory at the small village of Thakeham, near Storrington, filling bags with feed-pellets for pigs and turkeys. The weather, on the whole was miserable, the pay poor with the 40-hour basic being £15.45 less tax leaving my take home pay at £12.01 and to top it off, a general miners' strike led to power cuts and for a time the factory only ran at night. For me this was fine, as it meant I was paid overtime!

As 1972 progressed I decided I should explore Britain before I set off for Africa. Although I had now been here for two years, I had only really explored parts of London, Sussex, Kent and a small part of North Wales. In late January, along with Antipodean friends working in Storrington, I travelled in an old Ford Anglia 105E to the Isle of Wight for a weekend. The little Anglia, with its backward-sloping rear-window was rather cramped with 5 grown men squashed into it and, despite the weather, we had a great couple of days exploring as much of the Island as we could in the time available. At Easter I visited my friend Rick, with whom I had met on the Overland and with whom had travelled to Russia. Rick was then living in Liverpool with relations. I spent an interesting few days there, although again the weather was terrible; we visited Blackpool in the rain and on Easter Saturday went to the football, seeing Liverpool beat West Bromwich Albion 2 – nil at Annfield. The football experience, the only First (now Premier) Division match I have ever been to, was interesting. Along with some of Rick's Liverpool mates we were in the 'kop', a stand – literally – that could hold up to 30,000 spectators that had been named for the Boer War Battle of Spion Kop. The 'Kop' was famous for its singing, a 25,000-voice choir according to a LP record cover, with *You'll Never Walk Alone* being the signature tune. When Liverpool scored the spectators of the kop surged forward and there was no choice but to go with them, down several steps, then to be swept back with the return surge. It was quite an experience. After the match we went to the home of one of Rick's friends in the suburb of Kirkby. This had been part of the Liverpool slum-resettlement scheme and the relatively new apartment was rather tidy but I can remember being amazed that, other than a toilet and hand-basin, there was no bathroom and once a week the occupiers would go to a public bath-house.

At the beginning of May I left Storrington and caught an overnight bus from London to Edinburgh before continuing on to Oban on the west coast of Scotland. I had chosen Oban as a starting point as I wished first to visit the restored Abbey of St Columba on the little island of Iona. Next morning I first climbed up to McCaig's Folly, a large circular tower constructed of granite which had been built by a local philanthropist in the late 19th century to 'provide winter work for the local stone masons', and later that morning caught the ferry to Craignure on the Island of Mull. I then travelled by bus, entertained by a lively commentary on local history, to the little port of Fionnphort on the Sound of Iona. The weather was deteriorating as we crossed to the holy island in a small open boat. The Abbey on Iona has been reconstructed on the site of the original monastery which was founded in the 6th century by St. Columba, an Irish monk. This is said to be the earliest centre of Christianity in Britain and over the centuries the monastic community was devastated by the Vikings several times. The later Benedictine Monastery had been dismantled during the

Scottish Reformation in the late 16th century and the site was abandoned. Iona had a noticeable spiritual feel to it and I wandered, in the increasingly heavy rain, around Abbey and to the ancient burial ground where the ancient Celtic crosses looked mystical under the lowering, stormy sky. Many early kings of Scotland had been crowned on Iona and were buried here, including Macbeth. In was a rather wet crossing back to Fionnphort with the choppy waters of the Sound slopping over the gunwales and one or two of the Scottish lady passengers were becoming quite apprehensive by the time we reached the little port on Mull to reconnect with the bus back to Craignure. It was late evening when I finally got back to the Youth Hostel in Oban.

The next day I hitched a lift to Fort William from where I made my way to the Youth Hostel in Glen Nevis. I stayed here for two nights and on the first day hiked, with a German companion, to the top of Ben Nevis which is, at 1344 metres, the highest mountain in the British Isles. I found the walk quite reasonable, tiring in places but not an ordeal. The day started nice and clear with splendid views over Fort William and Loch Linnhe, but as we reached the snow-patches near the summit the "*mists came down obscuring the view. Strong gusts of wind made the going more difficult and eddies of driving ice didn't help either. The last half mile or so was across packed ice and we felt somewhat like Scott at the Antarctic as there was a virtual blizzard condition up there and visibility was about 20 yards.*" But I had reached the highest point on the British Isles.

The Isle of Skye now beckoned, and I headed to the small port of Mallaig, which I reached after walking about 8 miles before finally getting a ride. I caught the ferry to Armadale and made my way to the Youth Hostel in Broadford. The next day I hired a bicycle and cycled along a narrow picturesque country road to the small village of Elgol from where there are dramatic views of the Cuillin Mountains across Loch Scavaig.

I had travelled to Scotland in May as I had been told the weather was the best at this time of the year, and it didn't disappoint. I hitch-hiked from the Isle of Skye, via Inverness, to Carbisdale Castle Youth Hostel where I stayed for 3 nights. The Castle only dates from the early 20th century, having been built for a former Duchess of Sutherland after an acrimonious legacy settlement with her deceased husband's family and due to its situation in Ross-shire, just outside Sutherlandshire, it became known as the 'Castle of Spite'. During World War 2 it had been occupied by King Haakon VII who was in exile in Britain during the German occupation of Norway. In 1945 it was gifted to the Scottish Youth Hostel Association. The Castle is only a few kilometres from the small town of Bonar Bridge which was then on the main Inverness to Wick Highway. I walked from the main road and arrived early, well before the hostel's opening time of 5pm. Another traveller arrived, and we were sitting talking when we heard what sounded, to me, like a piper. I commented on this to my companion and he agreed that it did indeed sound like someone playing the bagpipes. We thought no more of it until the next morning when the warden of the hostel gave a tour of the castle. During the tour, he commented that ghosts were said to frequent the castle. A woman in white had been seen, as had soldiers from a centuries-old battle that had occurred on the castle site - and also a phantom piper! I looked at my companion of the previous day and he looked back at me and neither of us said a word!

I hitched north, first to the small town of Lairg where I waited quite some time before being picked up by a Dutch couple and taken across the bleak moors of Sutherlandshire to Tongue, an remote little crofting village dominated by the granite crags of Ben Loyal. That evening as I walked along the Kyle of Tongue to a local pub, the mists came down giving the area of air of mystery, just how I imagined the remote Highlands of Scotland to be. In the distance I could hear the booming of the wild North Atlantic swells on the coastal cliffs.

Next morning, I caught the local 'mail' bus to Scrabster, the port of Thurso, to make sure I would be in time to catch the ferry, the MV *St. Ola*, to Stromness on Orkney. It was here that I met Rob, a South African traveller who bounced a small rubber ball wherever he went. He was also travelling to Stromness and also intended staying at the Youth Hostel which was the old town hall and had just opened for the first time a few days earlier. It was a pleasant voyage in calm weather along a dramatic coast, past the monolithic sea stack known as the Old Man of Hoy and into tranquil Stromness Harbour in Scapa Flow. We soon found the new youth hostel and made friends with Bill the warden, a Scotsman and a self-styled Communist.

Over the next week Rob and I explored the area around Stromness and the town of Kirkwall. The ancient Neolithic sites of Skara Brae, the Ring of Brogar and the Standing Stones of Stenness were particularly fascinating. Skara Brae is a complete Neolithic settlement, the best preserved in Europe, in which could be seen basic dwellings, some complete with stone shelving and the outline of beds. No one else was here during our visit which made the site even more fascinating and allowed my imagination to run wild. I had visited Stonehenge, but these sites on Orkney, although smaller had, to me, much more mystique attached to them. Nearby is Maeshowe, a chambered Neolithic tomb which, like the other three sites, is believed to date from between 2500 and 3000BC. There are also Runic inscriptions carved by Viking treasure seekers on rock slabs within the ancient Maeshowe barrow. Kirkwall, which is the main town on Orkney, has an interesting Cathedral which dates from Viking times. Construction of the Romanesque Cathedral of St Magnus began in 1137 on the orders of Earl Rognvald Kolsson, the nephew of St. Magnus the Martyr after whom the church was named. Close by are the ruins of the Bishop's Palace and I spent some time in these two fascinating buildings.

During the week, Rob, Bill and I went on a couple of coastal walks out of Stromness where there is spectacular coastal scenery. The wild North Atlantic swells crash unimpeded onto steep rocky cliffs, creating inaccessible seastacks and sea caves. It was off this coast on a stormy night in 1916 that Lord Kitchener of Khartoum met his untimely end when the HMS *Hampshire*, taking him and his entourage to Russia, struck a German mine and sank almost immediately. Of the 749 people on board, only 12 survived. The inherent dangers of these cliffs were brought home during my stay when the Stromness lifeboat was called out early one morning. As the day progressed I could see little groups of people standing in shop doorways or on street corners conversing in hushed whispers. The entire community was concerned and when finally the lifeboat returned in the late afternoon the news wasn't good. Two local fishermen had perished when their fishing boat had capsized in heavy seas close inshore to these treacherous cliffs. On another day, Rob and I went walking along the coast of Scapa Flow, the sheltered body of water that provided a major anchorage for the British fleets during both the First and Second World Wars. It was here that the German High Sea fleet was scuttled in 1919 by its sailors, after having surrendered under the terms of the Armistice. Although no evidence now remains of this momentous event, we did scramble over a later wreck of a steel-hulled fishing boat cast up on the shore. It looked as if it may have been beached after an onboard fire.

It was now time to leave Orkney. A new ferry service had just begun operating from the small Orcadian settlement of St Margaret Hope direct to John

O'Groats on the northern tip of Scotland. I decided that this would be an ideal route. I took my leave of Bill and Rob, who was heading back to Scrabster, and hitched down to St. Margaret Hope, getting a ride all the way in a baker's van. The road crossed the Churchill Barriers, built as naval defences by Italian prisoners-of-war after a German U-boat had entered Scapa Flow through one of these channels and torpedoed the battleship HMS *Royal Oak* in October 1939. After a beer in St. Margaret Hope I caught the ferry, the MV *Pentalina,* across the turbulent waters of Pentland Firth. I remember Mr Bell, my Scottish primary school teacher, telling us that the Pentland Firth was among the most treacherous straits in the world. As I watched the malevolent eddies swirling around us as we headed to John O'Groats I thought of Mr Bell – 'You were quite right, sir!'

I spent a night at the Youth Hostel at John O'Groats and in the morning caught a bus to Wick before spending much of the afternoon trying to hitch hike south, hoping to reach Inverness. It wasn't that people would not pick me up – it was just that there were hardly any vehicles on the road, but I did eventually make it to Helmsdale, some 68 miles short of Inverness, where I spent the night at the small Youth Hostel. I had more success hitching the next day and got as far as Aviemore. Aviemore is a ski resort and climbing centre in the Cairngorms and, although early summer, there was still some snow in the mountains. I noted in my diary: '*I was disappointed in Aviemore. I had expected to find it in the mountains, but it's not, and it has been geared to tourism – a miniature Blackpool.'*

From Aviemore I hitched a ride straight through to Stirling. I spent the afternoon exploring the dramatically sited Stirling Castle and the nearby Church of the Holy Rude before checking into the Youth Hostel for the night. Next day I caught a bus to Edinburgh arriving just as a 21-gun salute was being fired from the Castle to mark the Queen's official birthday. I spent a couple of days exploring Edinburgh, mainly with Rob, the South African, whom I had last seen in Orkney. He was staying with friends in Edinburgh and they kindly took me along with them on a couple of sightseeing expeditions, including a trip out to the suburb of Musselburgh where Rob wanted to visit a camping exhibition.

In Edinburgh Castle I was particularly fascinated by the massive 15th century cannon known as Mons Meg. This huge bombard had been a gift to James II, King of Scotland from Philip the Good, Duke of Burgundy in 1454. Just outside the Castle I stopped for a beer at a pub called the 'Ensign Ewart'. I had also noticed the tomb of this soldier close to the castle. Ensign Charles Ewart was a soldier of the Royal North British Dragoons, better known as the 'Scots Greys', during the Battle of Waterloo when, in close fighting, he had captured the regimental eagle standard of the French 45th Regiment of the Line and lived to tell the tale: "*One made a thrust at my groin, I parried him off and cut him down through the head. A lancer came at me - I threw the lance off by my right side and cut him through the chin and upwards through the teeth. Next, a foot soldier fired at me and then charged me with his bayonet, which I also had the good luck to parry, and then I cut him down through the head"*.

While I was in the Ensign Ewart there was television coverage of the funeral of the Duke of Windsor, formerly King Edward VIII, who had passed away in Paris a few days earlier.

My next destination was Tynemouth which took me the better part of a day to reach. I would be staying for a few days with Lily, a cousin of my Dad. Lily had been our last contact with my father's family in the UK. Dad had been just six years old when his family had emigrated just after the First World War and he had never been back, but Lily, in later years, had kept up a correspondence first with my paternal grandmother and after her passing, with an aunt so I had been able to make contact. Aunt Lily, her retired husband Sid, and their neurotic dog Brindle – who took an immediate dislike to me – lived at Cullercoats, just a couple of miles from Tynemouth. I spent a very pleasant week with them, using the opportunity to explore the area. There was an interesting ruined Priory at Tynemouth right at the entrance to the River Tyne and one foggy morning I watched the North Sea ferry from Bergen in Norway emerge out of the murk and make its way into the River Tyne. The next day I wandered around Newcastle-upon-Tyne, crossing and re-crossing the river by different bridges and visiting the Museum of Science and

Engineering. I found the Civic Centre sculpture by David Wynne, personifying the River Tyne, particularly interesting. When I look back at my stay with Aunt Lily, my biggest regret was not finding out more about my father's family. Once Lily had passed on I had lost the last link with my father's UK side of the family about which I currently know very little.

Aunt Lily's daughter Marion kindly drove me to Middlesbrough. In increasingly deteriorating weather I had a look at the unusual Port Clarence Transporter Bridge, where vehicles and passengers are 'transported' in a 'gondola' across the River Tees to the Hartlepool road. As it was now raining heavily I caught a bus to Whitby, a place I had always wanted to visit mainly because of its association with Captain Cook and, consequently, with New Zealand. Whitby, situated on the River Esk, is a charming town and although the Museum with its Cook exhibits and the first ichthyosaurus fossil were interesting, it was the ruins of Whitby Abbey and the graveyard that really enthralled me. I stayed in the Youth Hostel right next to the ruins and it wasn't until later that I discovered the Abbey ruins have an association with Bram Stoker's *Dracula* and I can see that the author chose his venue well. At night the ruins were quite eerie and during the heavily-overcast day there was a certain mystique about the ruins. When I re-read *Dracula* a few years later, I was immediately able to associate parts of the story with Whitby Abbey.

I hitch-hiked out of Whitby and was given a lift by a lorry driver all the way to York. I was impressed with York, particularly the magnificent Gothic Minster which looked resplendent in the early summer sunlight, complimented by yellow laburnums which were now flowering in the cathedral gardens. Unfortunately, there was a lot of reconstruction and strengthening work going on inside with scaffolding spoiling the magnificence of the interior. I circumambulated the old York city walls, scrambled up to Clifford's Tower which is all that now remains of York Castle, and wandered through the Shambles where once the city's meat dealers plied their trade. I photographed the red Stonegate Devil outside a former printer's shop in Stonegate, making sure I didn't look into his eyes! This little fellow got the blame when any type was misspelt when going to Press.

I passed on quickly through Lincoln to Coventry, where I had a look at the modern cathedral of Sir Basil Spence which had replaced the one destroyed by German bombers in 1940. After a night at the youth hostel in Stratford-upon-Avon, I hitched to Chepstow and walked across the then relatively new River Severn Suspension Bridge which had been open for just over 5 years. I can remember feeling the bridge quivering and trembling as traffic went by, probably accentuated by the gusty winds of that day. I spent a couple of nights in the delightful Georgian city of Bath before heading to Wells in Somerset.

Near Wells are the ruins of the Abbey of Glastonbury, which then had a much lower profile than it now does. It was here I first became acquainted with the colourful legends surrounding King Arthur and his Knights of the Round Table. I was to hear much more of these traditions as I journeyed further into the West Country. Glastonbury's connection with King Arthur stems from the timely discovery by monks in 1191 of a grave containing the body of a man and woman – reputedly Arthur and Guinevere – upon which was a lead cross bearing the inscription in Latin: *Hic jacet sepultus inclitus rex Arthurus in insula Avalonia* ("*Here lies interred the famous King Arthur on the Isle of Avalon*"). This discovery gave rise to the belief that Glastonbury was also mythical Avalon. The grave site can still be seen, but the remains, re-interred beneath the high altar, were lost during the dissolution of the Monasteries in the reign of Henry VIII. Another interesting legend is that Christian Glastonbury dates back to the first century AD when Joseph of Arimathea, after donating his prepared tomb for the burial of Jesus in Jerusalem, became a wandering mendicant, travelling throughout Europe before arriving in Glastonbury. Upon sticking his staff in the ground, it sprang into life becoming the 'Glastonbury thorn', a type of hawthorn which is unusual in that it is said to flower twice each year. He was also said to have brought and hidden the elusive and mysterious Holy Grail, thus Glastonbury became a central part of Arthurian legend. I was virtually alone as I wandered around the Abbey ruins, through the remains of the old church and the more intact Monks' kitchen.

I stopped for a couple of days at the Youth Hostel in Instow on the River Torridge opposite a small fishing village with the delightful name of Appledore. I travelled by local bus to the nearby beach resort of Westward Ho! It was the name that had brought me here, as I knew the beach had been named in the 19th century after the novel by Charles Kingsley who hailed from the nearby town of Bideford. *Westward Ho!* the novel, is a good rip-roaring story of the sea and exploration set in Elizabethan times with close association with this area of Devon:

And on the 15th November 1583 dropped down from Bideford Quay to Appledore Pool the tall ship Rose, *with a hundred men on board (for sailors packed close in those days), beef, pork, biscuit, and good ale (for ale went to sea always then) in abundance, four culverins on her main deck, her poop and forecastle well fitted with swivels of every size, and her racks so full of muskets, calivers, long-bows, pikes, and swords, that all agreed so well-appointed a ship had never sailed "out over Bar."*

From Westward Ho! I walked along the country by-lanes through a locality with the delightful name of Diddywell to Appledore where a full-sized replica of Sir Francis Drake's *Golden Hind* was being built. Unfortunately, the boatshed was closed so I caught the small on-demand open ferry across the river Torridge back to Instow.

I hitch-hiked and walked to the pretty coastal fishing village of Boscastle in Cornwall, which has a Museum of Witchcraft but, more importantly, is the beginning of a 5-mile walking track along the spectacular Cornish coastline to Tintagel, an area steeped in Arthurian Legend. I began the coastal walk in misty rain, passing through Rocky Valley, an impressive slate canyon eroded by the small Trevillet River. The rain fortunately did clear and though wet from the knees down, I enjoyed the walk immensely even though I was carrying my back-pack.

In Tintagel I checked into the Youth Hostel which had once been the office of a slate mine and was situated on a spectacular site high above the rugged Cornish coast. I immediately liked Tintagel which, in 1972, was not yet widely visited. In fact I had only heard of the town a few days before during a discussion with fellow travellers at the Bath youth hostel. The small bay at Tintagel is dominated by a large headland upon which are the remains of an old castle, most of which dates from the 12th century but earlier ruins, perhaps a Celtic monastery and a former fortress, date back to the 6th century, which certainly fits in with the time frame of Arthurian legend. According to the 12th century historian, Geoffrey of Monmouth, Uther Pendragon, a king of post-Roman Britain, had a fixation with Ygerna, wife of Gorlois, Duke of Cornwall. With the connivance of the magician Merlin: *By my drugs I know how to give you the precise appearance of Gorlois, so that you will resemble him in every respect.* The disguised Uther Pendragon travelled to Tintagel Castle while Gorlois was away at war: *The King spent that night with Ygerna and satisfied his desire by making love with her. ... That night she conceived Arthur, the most famous of men, who subsequently won great renown by his outstanding bravery.* Next morning news was received that Gorlois had been killed in battle. Uther Pendragon then took Tintagel Castle and married Ygerna, thus legitimising Arthur's birth.

Beneath the Tintagel Castle headland is a large sea cave known locally as Merlin's Cave. Uther had died before Arthur's birth and according to Alfred, Lord Tennyson in *The Idylls of the King*, Merlin is said to have rescued the baby Arthur here:

> *Wave after wave, each mightier than the last,*
> *Till last, a ninth one, gathering half the deep*
> *And full of voices, slowly rose and plunged*
> *Roaring, and all the wave was in a flame:*
> *And down the wave and in the flame was borne*
> *A naked babe, and rode to Merlin's feet,*
> *Who stoopt and caught the babe, and cried 'The King!*

*Here is an heir for Uther!'
And the fringe
Of that great breaker,
sweeping up the strand,
Lash'd at the wizard as he
spake the word,
And all at once round him
rose in fire,
So that the child and he
were clothed in fire.*

The cave, accessible only at low tide, spurred my imagination and I wrote in my diary: '*It is not terribly hard to picture the bearded Merlin in his robes and peaked hat, casting spells over a cauldron in the cave.*' Guess I had been overly influenced by Disney in those days! I spent a couple of days exploring the castle ruins, Tintagel village and this dramatic section of the Cornish coast. Tintagel was just beginning to cash in on the Arthurian legends and there was a rather tacky 'sword' stuck in a stone, alongside a bar called, tastelessly, 'Excali-bar'! The old stone-slab post office, then a small museum, was an interesting structure. The days were sunny and warm, and I spent time along the cliff tops near the youth hostel, scrambling down one morning to a small rocky bay for a dip in the Atlantic. It was a very quick dip as I was surprised at how cold the water was. It was also the first time I had come upon small globules of crude oil, washed up on the rocks. This was a legacy of the *Torrey Canyon* disaster which took place on a reef off the coast of Cornwall in 1967. The wreck of this super tanker was the world's first major environmental oil spill and, to date, Britain's worst. Five years on, small amounts of the tar-like crude oil still remained on this otherwise pristine coast.

It was slow hitching from Tintagel to Hayle where I spent a couple of nights at the Youth Hostel. While here I, along with an Australian and Mary, an English girl, caught a bus to the iconic artists' town of St. Ives which, of course, I knew from the nursery-rhyme riddle. My impressions were mixed, and I wrote in my diary at the time: *'The town and harbour of St. Ives are very picturesque but unfortunately commercialism has taken over here. Crowds of holidaymakers and even a colony of hippies come here making the place unpleasant to be in. The few sheltered beaches are jam-packed with people, all in behind their little coloured canvas windbreaks. On seeing one beach the Australian, who'd only been in Britain a couple of months, just stopped and exclaimed "I don't believe it." then started laughing. Mary just said "This is what makes me ashamed to be English."*

Next day Mary and I hitched a ride, first to the Youth Hostel at St. Just where we dropped off our gear. The same driver then took us all the way to Land's End which had been my main objective since arriving by ferry at John O'Groats. I had now completed the iconic land route between John O'Groats to Land's End. It was a calm day as Mary and I stood on Land's End, looking across the silky waters to the Longships lighthouse and the more distant Isles of Scilly, just visible through the sea mists. We walked back along the coastal path, stopping for about an hour at Sennen Cove, before arriving back at the Youth Hostel in St. Just. The next day the weather was not too good but there was one more place I felt I had to visit in Cornwall, mainly because of its name. This was Mousehole, pronounced '*morezell*', not far from Penzance. Mary and I, after a combination of hitch-hiking and walking in increasingly heavy rain, reached the little village soaking wet. Mousehole was said to be a typical Cornish village of particular beauty, but as it was now raining steadily we saw nothing of the village and sought sanctuary in a local pub in an attempt to dry off. We had a pint or two and a real Cornish pasty which, quite frankly, was disappointing. I do remember two local men sitting in the next cubicle chatting to each other. It took me sometime to figure that they were, in fact, speaking English in a very definite, thick Cornish brogue. I knew the Cornish language was no longer spoken and hadn't been for a couple of centuries. It was a resident of Mousehole, Dolly Pentreath, who was the last recorded native speaker in the 18th century. We caught a bus back to Penzance and on to St Just.

It was now time to think about heading back to Sussex where once again I was to work the harvest. Mary and I spent a slow day hitching first to Golant where we spent the night in the Youth Hostel and then on to the city of Exeter where we parted company, as Mary was heading back to London before flying to Canada. I spent a day in Exeter before hitching, without any long waits, to Winchester, the former capital of Saxon England where there is a statue of King Alfred the Great in the centre of town. In the Great Hall of Winchester Castle hangs the 'Round Table' of King Arthur and his Knights, although it is now known that this dates from the 13th century and was painted in its present form on the orders of Henry VIII. It did seem rather apt that this 'relic' was to be my last connection with the Arthurian legends on this journey.

The Youth Hostel in Winchester was the old city mill where the waters of the millrace raced through the men's bathroom. I did, of course, visit Winchester Cathedral and was intrigued by the story of William Walker, the diver 'who saved the Cathedral'. When the Cathedral had been built in the 11th century, the walls of the nave had been supported on a couple of layers of thick beech tree logs over a peat bed, which had compressed and sunk over the centuries leading to a serious cracking of the nave walls by the early 20th century. To fix the problem, the walls had to be underpinned and the only way to do this was with the services of a diver:

> '*To pass from the work of restoration into the nave of the Cathedral is to enter another world. The rolling glory of the* Te Deum *echoes through the vaulted space as it did in the days of William of Wykeham. The last* Amen *is sung, and the choir and clergy pass slowly and silently into the vestry. Outside the foreman blows his whistle. The great helmet*

of the diver with its staring goggle eyes, appears above the brink of the shaft, and the diver is helped out of his slimy, dripping shell. And soon the choristers and workmen mingle beneath the shadow of the Cathedral.'

Over five years William Walker is estimated to have handled 25,800 bags of concrete, 114,900 concrete blocks and some 900,000 bricks. An incredible feat when one considers that a diver's outfit in those days weighed around 200 pounds and he was working in a complete watery darkness in a graveyard. He well deserved the monument to him in the Cathedral.

Back in Sussex I was now working and saving for my journey back to New Zealand but not without a few deviations. I visited the 1972 Farnborough Airshow with Bill and Vi with whom I was staying once again. The highlight of the Show was a low-level pass over the airfield by Concorde 002. The world's first effective supersonic aircraft, Concorde was then still in its testing phase and was not to enter commercial service until 1977.

Valerie, my sister, arrived in London late in the summer of 1972 and she accompanied me on one last visit to Saumur to work the grape-harvest at Chateau de Chaintre. I also convinced Keith Hawkings, another New Zealander, who was also working at Sullington, to come down to France with Valerie and me. Keith ended up meeting Holly, a girl from Alaska, who was cycling around France. They ended up marrying and moved to Alaska. I was to visit them in Anchorage some years later. Valerie and I returned to England by way of Paris, Reims and Luxembourg.

I would now work continuously on Sullington Manor Farm until my departure from England in September 1973. Although farm labouring was one of the lowest paid jobs in Britain, I was able to save more here than I could on a higher wage in London. Accommodation on the farm was provided as were all vegetables. I just had to buy the meat I needed. Also at certain times of the year there was quite a lot of overtime, particularly during the harvest and at the seasonal planting times. Besides cereal crops – wheat, barley and oats – Sullington Manor Farm ran beef cattle on about half of its 500 acres. We also had gardens which provided fresh vegetables for a family-owned hotel in Hove, near Brighton. We also grew potatoes and strawberries for the general public who purchased direct. I always remember one little incident, and Keith has always reminded me of it whenever we meet. Our boss, the farm owner John, had a very bad stutter. John had been busy preparing a sign for the sale of the potatoes. One morning we noticed the sign advertising '*potatatoes*'. John was standing close by and Keith, grinning, asked him who had written the sign. John stuttered "I ... I did" and Keith guffawed loudly. John stalked off, probably embarrassed. Keith later said he knew his laughter was insensitive but he just couldn't help it. I knew what he meant…

The Boxing Day shoot on Sullington Manor Farm, Sussex. December 1971

The Neolithic ruins of Skara Brae, on the Scottish island of Orkney, May 1972

Chapter 11 Across the Sahara to Kano

I had decided to return to New Zealand by another epic Overland journey and this time, travelled through Africa with a company called Intertrek. I would travel with them as far as Nairobi and then I would make my way down to Johannesburg where I was hoping to find work for about six months before catching a ship from Cape Town back to Auckland in the middle of 1974. The Intertrek office and operations base was in the Battersea High Street south of the Thames. In my last few weeks in the UK, I had to go up to London several times to obtain visas, vaccinations - for smallpox, cholera, typhoid, paratyphoid and yellow-fever - and to sort out other documentation.

This was a time when IRA bombers were active in London and after the Intertrek tour briefing on a Saturday in early September 1973 I headed to Victoria station to catch the train back to Pulborough, the station closest to Storrington. I was a little early so decided to have a meal at a nearby Wimpy restaurant. As I was walking back I noticed people streaming out of the station, then police, fire brigade and ambulances began arriving. Just a few minutes earlier a bomb had exploded in Victoria station, destroying the season-ticket office. I don't think anyone was killed but there were a several injuries from flying debris. Trains were of course delayed for several hours. Twice, in the next week, I was caught up in bomb scares, once at Redhill station where I was transferring to visit my sister Valerie who was working in Hever in Kent, and the second time my carriage on the train to Pulborough was evacuated due to an unattended bag. It all seemed rather ironic, as during the African briefing we had been warned about the possible political dangers we could expect on the expedition through Africa and here it was, happening in England!

Although the last week was spent mainly hand-weeding stinging nettles out of the manor garden, I was rather sad to be leaving Sullington Manor farm and surreptitiously wiped away a tear as I looked across the fields for the last time as I walked up Sullington Lane to the bus stop. It was the 23rd September 1973, and that afternoon I set off on Intertrek's first trans-African Expedition to Nairobi. We had one Bedford 4-wheel drive truck, specially modified for the rigours of Africa, having been fitted with two 120-gallon tanks – one for diesel, the other for water. It would have a reputed range of around 1400 miles. Sand tracks were also strapped on each side. We also had an attendant 4-wheel drive Land Rover carrying extra jerrycans of water and fuel.

After a night crossing from Dover to Zeebrugge, we drove quickly through to Paris where we had to stop a day while Keith Mitchell, our expedition leader, had to sort out some visa problems. It gave me a last chance to look around Paris. We were staying at the Bois de Boulogne camping ground on the edge of the city. One of our fellow travellers was a young lady from the US.

Jane, a likeable lady, was a real Texan in many respects and had a rather pronounced drawl. Several of us had just returned from the city when we saw Jane approaching with an obviously American couple, the male wearing the distinctive checked trousers that were in vogue with American tourists. Jane had told us earlier that she would be meeting friends here in Paris. Charlie, a hard-bitten Yorkshireman, looked across at the approaching threesome and said to us, under his breath: "*What's the betting this guy's name is either Homer or Elmer!*" Jane approached us with a cheery smile, saying: "*Hi, yo'all I'd like yo'all to meet Elmer and Betty.*" She couldn't work out why there was suppressed laughter all round. They were, in fact, a very pleasant couple.

We drove quickly down through France and Spain, spending our last night in Europe at a camping ground on the beach at Algeciras looking across at the bay to the Rock of Gibraltar. The following morning, as the sun rose, the Rock was starkly silhouetted against a vivid orange sky. We crossed, by ferry, from Algeciras to the Spanish Moroccan port of Ceuta and the African journey began in earnest.

Africa was to be so different from Asia. In late 1973, the Dark Continent was not without its problems but still pretty safe. Idi Amin, with his eccentricities, was in control of Uganda, so that was an area to be avoided, and also, unbeknown to us, as we set off into the Sahara, tensions between the Israelis, the Egyptians and other Arab nations increased to breaking point resulting in the

Yom Kippur War. There were also a number of lesser political and religious concerns that we had to be aware of, but during my journeying through Africa over the next 9 months, I was neither threatened nor felt threatened.

Our route from Ceuta first took us into the Rif Mountains, a rather attractive coastal range inhabited by Berber tribesmen, which extended to the border with Algeria. It took us about 3 hours to complete formalities to enter Algeria and we drove on to Oran, the country's second largest city. We were parked in the city centre when a group of young men approached us and started telling us 'We want peace, just peace.' We thought this strange but agreed with them saying we wanted the same, which of course was true. We wondered what this was all about, but on looking back through my diaries I noticed that this incident took place on 4 October 1973, just two days before the outbreak of the Yom Kippur hostilities. Tensions must have been building in the previous days, and as we had had no access to English-language newspapers, we were completely ignorant as to the international situation. We were to hear nothing more about the war until we had crossed the Sahara and reached Agadez in Niger about three weeks later.

The Sahara crossing was, to me, the highlight of the African trip. There is something about deserts that I love. It is the dryness of the landscape, the spectacular barrenness of the countryside where, to use the words of the poet Percy Bysshe Shelley: *'the lone level sands stretch far away'*. The Sahara shattered all my preconceptions of a desert. Far from being a vast area of featureless sand dunes and nothing else, I found the countryside was remarkably varied. The sand seas only occupied a small area of our crossing. Much of the Sahara consisted of rugged rocky mountains, such as the Tassili N'Ajjer, which although lacking hardly any form of vegetation somehow seems to support an amazingly large population. I remember one incident when we were deep in the desert. We had been driving all day, having not seen another vehicle or passed through any form of settlement. Several of us were sitting on a dune well above our camp site in what was a very black night. I thought I glimpsed, from the corner of my eye, a slight flicker of light in the next valley, as if someone had lit a cigarette. I immediately dismissed it thinking my eyes were playing tricks. Half an hour later we had returned to our camp, scaring our rostered 'guards' in the process – they hadn't realised some of the group were not in camp - and settled in for the night. Just a short time later two shadowy spectre-like figures ambled into the camp. This time the guards thought it was another attempt to scare them until a voice called out: *"H-hang on, guys, they're real!"* The two intruders were Tuaregs, the nomads of this part of the Sahara and, out of curiosity, were paying us a friendly visit. It appeared we were camped by one of their tribal wells. Language was a barrier, but we were able to communicate in pidgin French, and after offering them a cup of tea, they disappeared happily into the desert as silently as they had appeared.

As we drove into the Sahara, towns just seemed to appear out of the desert. Why were they here? No doubt water was the key factor and places such as Tiaret, Laghouart, Ghardaia, and Ouargla would once have been on caravan routes. We stopped at the market in Ouargla which was full of what are colloquially known as 'desert roses'. These are gypsum crystals naturally welded together into rose-like shapes, some quite large. Many of these were for sale with a few other uninspiring crafts. I commented, more than once in my diary that I wondered how people survived out here: '*Herds of goats and the odd Tuareg or two seem to appear in almost every small area of tussock which appears capable of supporting nothing!*'

In the desert south of Ouargla we passed the oil flares of the refinery of Hassi Messaoud and the next day, out of the heat and sand of the Grand Erg Oriental we came upon a cluster of small huts, as remote from civilisation as could be found anywhere. This was the tiny settlement of Bel Guebbour, a refuelling stop along the road which stretches off into the shimmering mirages of an even bleaker, more barren region of the Sahara. Sleepy lethargic Algerian men sat or squatted in shady doorways; we never saw any women. In the cool interior of a hut which seemed to double as the village shop, one of the group asked, without much hope, for a beer. Beer! We had hardly seen a bottle since we had been in the country and it was also Ramadan, the Moslem period of abstinence. *Bier*, no problem said the sleepy shopkeeper and pulled an ice-cold beer from the depths of his refrigerator. We were amazed – here in the middle of nowhere in the depths of the Sahara we were able to purchase a beer – and a cold one at that! Just a few kilometres out of Bel Guebbour we found a sulphurous, artesian spring with a concrete trough which gave us a welcome opportunity to wash, watched on by a number of bemused camels.

As we drove further into the desert, the settlements became more basic with places like Fort Polynac, now called Ilizi, and Fort Gardel having been outposts of the French Foreign Legion. Sparse huts and nomad tents had sprung up around the original forts and, over time, a small trading town would form. I remember Ilizi having a main street, replete with pavements and relatively modern street lighting, which did not now work as the lights were broken or just had wires dangling from the standards. There was one shop from which I bought a small tin of sweetened condensed milk. Lethargic Tuareg, in their signature bright blue garments, turbans and veils, lay or sat in the shade of walls, or house doorways, sheltering from the hot midday desert sun.

After leaving Ilizi, and having first pushed our vehicles through a large sand drift, we began to climb up into the rugged interior mountains of the central Sahara known as the Tassili N'Ajjer. Rather than being a true mountain range, the Tassili N'Ajjer is, in fact, a high plateau of around 7000 feet (2,100+ metres) stretching across much of south-east Algeria. The name means the Plateau of the Goats. As we progressed into the abject barrenness, the landscape became more and more spectacular with rocky mesas, rugged canyons and weirdly eroded conical hills. One evening several of us climbed a nearby hill to watch a spectacular full moon rise over this 'lunar landscape', where the *'desert ends and the mountains begin in a weird series of islands – devoid of vegetation.'* At the time I likened the Tassili to a Salvador Dali backdrop and imagined that this is what Tolkein's 'Mordor' from the *Lord of the Rings* would have looked like. I first read Tolkein's inspirational books while I was working in Sullington. This was almost 30 years before the trilogy was filmed in my homeland of New Zealand where the stark volcanic landscape of Mt Ruapehu and the volcanic cone of Ngauruhoe became 'Mordor' and Mt Doom respectively.

We drove out of the Tassili just before we reached Fort Gardel, and would now be skirting the plateau which was on our left. Fort Gardel was a sad place, hardly a town, just two or three huts with their lethargic inhabitants. As we headed towards the oasis town of Djanet on the edge of the Tassili, our truck hit a hole in the desert obscured by wind-blown sand. There was an almighty bump and it was immediately apparent something was wrong. It turned out that a half shaft had bent and we would no longer be able to use four-wheel drive – not an ideal situation to be in, in the heart of the Sahara! After makeshift repairs and a night in the desert, we limped on towards Djanet. The next morning, in the distance, we saw a caravan of around 30 camels making its way towards the town. This was an age-old spectacle and was the only camel caravan we saw in the Sahara. The following morning, moving like spectres in the early morning light, I saw the Tuareg guides leading the camels through the date palms of Djanet, close to our camp site.

We were in Djanet Oasis for three days while our road crew made further repairs to the damaged half-shaft. Unfortunately, they were unable to restore the truck's 4-wheel drive capability. This required more specialist attention than was available in Djanet, so we knew we would be in for a lot of pushing and shoving and the sand tracks would be getting a lot of use, as we headed south into the Hogar. Although there was not much to do in Djanet, it certainly wasn't an unpleasant town. The days were hot and the nights cold. We were usually awoken early by the roaring of a camel or two being slaughtered to provide fresh meat for the town. I found camel meat to be rather tough, no matter how it was cooked; goats' meat tended to be more palatable. A hill at the back of the town gave us a good view across the oasis and into the treeless ruggedness of the Tassili N'Ajjer.

After leaving Djanet, we backtracked to Fort Gardel where we refilled our jerrycans with water from a traditional well. The 'buckets' consisted of rubber scoops, made from tyre inner tubes, and as one was lowered, a full 'bucket' was hauled up – easy, anyone could do it! A group of Tuareg women were filling goatskins when we arrived, and they certainly made the process look easy. With great hilarity they watched our amateur attempts, usually losing most of the little water that was in our 'buckets' on the way up! Eventually they felt sorry for us and with even more hilarity showed us how it should be done and our jerrycans were soon filled. As we approached the Hogar Mountains, the desert became even more inhospitable. In these mountains there is evidence, in the form of Mesolithic rock art dating back as far as 8000BC, that the whole Sahara was greener and wetter. We passed an old abandoned Foreign Legion fort where I noted at the time that I wondered what the legionnaires would have had to have done to be posted here! Evenings in the Hogar were very pleasant. One evening: '*I walked alone to the top of a hill nearby just after sunset. It is quite an experience to sit upon a hill in the desert and listen to the silence. This time of the day the hills take on a purply sheen which gives the countryside a fairy-tale effect. These nights in the desert are something to remember.*'

As we drove through the Hogar we stopped at several small Tuareg settlements looking for *l'eau potable* for our jerrycans. This could be quite difficult as I noted: '*Tuaregs were rather friendly but it appears they drank from the rather stagnant pools used for washing, bathing and irrigation. The kids here are rather charming, each shaking our hand and greeting us with "ça va". We finally managed to fill four jerrycans from a reasonably clear irrigation ditch and received a gift of three tomatoes from a local Tuareg*'.

We eventually arrived in the town of Tamanrasset, a most welcome respite from the barrenness of the Hogar: '*To have fresh bread again, still warm from the oven, was bliss, as was a cold orange drink and fresh biscuits.*' Tammanrasset, situated virtually on the Tropic of Cancer, is the largest town in southern Algeria and although still some 400 kilometres from the border with Niger, we had to complete Algerian immigration and customs formalities here. I celebrated my 25th birthday the day we left Tamanrasset, a very quiet affair with no alcohol as we were camped out in the desert. We had to cross a flat featureless expanse of sandy desert and it was hot – I described the wind as coming from a 'blast furnace!' We were entering the area known as the Sahel, then in the throes of a severe drought and we began seeing more and more camel bones scattered in the desert. We officially crossed the border into Niger just south of In Guezzam, a motley conglomeration of mud huts and Tuareg tents, but we had to travel another 25 kilometres into the Republic to complete border formalities.

The Republic of Niger, not to be confused with Nigeria, had been part of the territory of French West Africa until its Independence in 1960. As we headed into Niger I noted that we were entering '*the most featureless, trackless waste that we have yet seen; only the odd sand dune and, of course, many mirages to break the monotony of this treeless waste. Both the Landrover and the lorry got bogged in sand, but we managed to extract them without too much difficulty.*' The first town we came to was Arlit, founded just 4 years earlier when a large uranium mine had been opened in the vicinity. It was here that we saw, in a back street, the first signs of the International Sahel famine relief with sacks of sorghum being distributed – 'a gift from the people of the USA'. It did look, however, as if they were being sold! As we headed south more stunted scrub and the rondavels, or beehive huts, of Equatorial Africa became more common.

We arrived in the town of Agadez to find that while we had been crossing the Sahara, the Yom Kippur War had been fought between the Israelis and the Arab Nations led by the Egyptians. The war was now over but the political aftermath and the resultant oil crisis was just beginning. The centre of Agadez is dominated by the Grand Mosque, an interesting mud brick construction which dates from the early 16th century. In reality this town marked the end of our Saharan crossing and as we progressed into the Sahel, which was just getting over a devastating drought, the countryside became greener. We were travelling through what I remember from my schooldays as being savannah. First stunted acacia thorn bushes became more frequent, then more areas of crop cultivation, more villages with beehive huts and increasing numbers of long-horned cattle and horses with fewer camels. People were changing too and we were now entering Hausa country.

The border crossing into Nigeria was south of the town of Zinder and we headed on to the major city of

Kano, then the second largest in Nigeria. After the places we had travelled through over the last three weeks, Kano was a welcome respite with still a few vestiges of British colonial rule. We joined the Kano Club for our time here. It gave us access to bars, a restaurant, swimming pool and a library. On the first night a group of us ate at the Club – pawpaw, steak chips and salad finished with banana jelly at a cost of around 75p (about $1.10US), followed of course by a few beers. Rather a contrast to the weevil infested flour, purchased in Agadez, that we had used to make pancakes on the last couple of mornings – at least the weevils gave us extra protein!

Kano is predominantly Islamic and Ramadan, the Moslem period of fasting, had just ended. As is traditional the local Hausa and Fulani chieftains were in town for the annual Durbar where they pay homage to the Emir of Kano. For two days, colourful ceremonies and parades roiled around the streets and squares of the city. We were privileged to see several of these interesting processions including one outside the Emir's palace. After parading through the streets the Emir, along with his sons and bodyguard, installed himself outside the Palace. Groups of horsemen, each representing their villages and resplendent in robes of brilliant reds, blues, greens, yellows, turquoise, purples, silver and black, accompanied by a cacophony of sound – one could hardly call it music - from drums and ridiculously long wind instruments, would peel away from the main body and dash, at speed, across the palace square. Reining in just a few feet from the Emir to offer their allegiance, they then sedately trotted back around the edge of the square to rejoin the main group. All the time colourfully-clad musketeers were discharging their ancient jezails skyward. It really was an unforgettably colourful experience.

The next morning, after climbing to the top of the minaret of the Great Mosque of Kano, I explored the market of the old town, '*a system of mud huts, rickety stalls, open sewers, heaps of rubbish, dead rats, colourful people and an assortment of dogs, lizards, goats and donkeys … the stench leaves a lot to be desired.*' I again came upon another of the colourful processions as the Emir paraded through the streets of Kano, being seen by his subjects. It was hard to believe that we were in the latter half of the 20th century.

Tuaregs with their camels in the dates palms of Djanet Oasis, Algeria October 1973

The Grand Mosque of Agadez in the Republic of Niger, October 1973

Chapter 12 Central Africa to Nairobi

After leaving Kano our route over the next two days took us through the more fertile and populated areas of northern Nigeria to the city of Maiduguri, a pleasant town with a marked European influence, where we cleared Nigerian immigration and customs. Before crossing the border into northern Cameroon, we shopped at the small town of Bama. The people here were predominantly Fulani and there is a large colourful market '*smelling strongly of spices and reeking of dried fish which lay in rows on the ground.*' I also noted that the colourfully dressed women had teeth that were '*horribly stained*' presumably by betel. We found we needed visas to enter the former French colony of Cameroon. These could be obtained at the border and there was a short delay while these were sorted. After entering the country, we camped not far from the border.

After shopping in the small market town of Mokolo, we followed a secondary road that ran parallel to the Nigerian border. This road took us into the Mandara Mountains which is a geologically interesting and picturesque area of volcanic plugs of which the largest, at 1224 metres, is Kapsiki Peak, near the village of Rhumsiki. In 1973 this area was little visited but is now one of the most popular tourist destinations in Cameroon. As we drove along a dusty, gravel road through this fascinating area, the opening lines of Bilbo's song, as he leaves the Shire, in *The Fellowship of the*

Rings, first volume of J.R.R. Tolkein's *Lord of the Rings* trilogy, sprang to mind. It still does when I look at the photo I took at the time:

> "The Road goes ever on and on
> Down from the door where it began.
> Now far ahead the Road has gone,
> And I must follow, if I can."

We stopped in the large town of Garoua. At the Post Office I was rather surprised to see a poster advertising a film: *Nouvelle-Zélande terre des Maoris – un grand film en couleur,* sponsored by Cameroon Airlines and UTA, the French airline which did, at the time, fly into Auckland. The poster showed an old Maori woman with a chin tattoo or *moko*. It seemed rather incongruous to be in the heart of darkest Africa and to come across a poster advertising a film about the natives of one's own country! We stopped just out of town at the Bénoué River for much of the afternoon. The truck had developed an oil leak and the road crew were working on it. The Bénoué River was fairly wide and judging from the height of the bridge and the steep banks, it must regularly flood. At the moment it was quite low and I noted in my diary: '*The river is somewhat dirty but not too bad. I didn't swim but washed my hair and some clothes.*' The 'dirtiness' was more from the reddish earth of the area through which the river flowed rather than from pollution.

As we drove through Cameroon, we were entering what could be called 'stereotype' Africa. Vegetation became a lot lusher with the higher rainfall. We started to see wildlife such as monkeys, and brightly-coloured birds. When we reached the town of Ngaoundéré, I was on cook detail and we went shopping for meat in the local market. I mentioned in my diary that we *'purchased a nice piece of meat from a fly-infested stall'*, and I can remember shaking the meat to get rid of the flies to see what the cut looked like. We always cooked the meat well so no one on the trip ever had any adverse effects from the over attentions of the order *Diptera*!

The Cameroons has some very attractive scenery and we spent the best part of a morning swimming at Lake Tison, a small, beautiful crater lake with clear blue water. The Chutes du Tello is a large waterfall with a large fern-adorned cave behind the curtain of water, into which some of us scrambled. I wrote that it was quite an experience to be able to stand in a cave behind a waterfall. Driving down a back road we came to the small village of Belel, the dust in the market being extremely red. I noted in my diary that: *'the natives were very friendly and gave the impression that we were the first white people they had seen for some time.'* The road out of Belel to Meiganga was the worst we had encountered so far on the trip: *'the road steadily got worse until it appeared to be a river during the rains as well as the road – progress was very slow with much bumping and rocking from side to side. Tall elephant grass flanks either side of the track.'*

We crossed into the Central African Republic with surprisingly little delay but were directed to a nearby local hospital to have our vehicles disinfected, no one was quite sure against what! A doctor and his assistant eventually turned up and sprinkled disinfectant throughout the interiors of both our Bedford and the Landrover. The Central African Republic was then under the control of 'President for Life' Jean-Bédel Bokassa. It was still a number of years before his excesses and extravagances, as the self-styled Emperor of the Central African Empire, led to his deposition. In 1973 he was still relatively unknown on the world stage but was one of three dictators in central Africa who achieved notoriety in the 1970s – the other two being Mobutu Sese Seko of Zaïre and Idi Amin of Uganda.

We were now in the Bantu ethnic area of Africa and I had noticed the appearance of the people was changing again. One night, just after we had entered the Central African Republic, on the night of a full moon, we were camping on a village football field not far from the town of Bouar. As the moon rose *'we could hear drums and singing from a neighbouring village so a group of us set out along the road and came upon a group of Africans, mainly children, dancing to the sound of tomtoms and whistles. The children became quite excited by our presence and the whole scene was one of unreality – the throbbing jungle beat under a full moon, a scene of complete disorganisation with kids, some quite young, milling around, bobbing up and down to the beat. It really was quite an experience.'*

We stopped at the picturesque Boali Falls, before spending two days in Bangui, the country's capital. Here we obtained visas and had the vehicles serviced in preparation for the rigorous drive through Zaïre. Bangui was a modern and reasonably well-planned city without much of real interest. On the second morning I wandered down to the Ubangui River, a wide tributary of the River Congo which serves as the border between the Central African Republic and Zaïre, as the Democratic Republic of the Congo was then known. I sat there for some time watching life go by. Tree branches and other matted vegetable debris drifted past. Locals in the traditional dugouts, some with outboard motors, plied to and fro and a couple of fishermen, skilfully tossing their weighed, circular throw-nets, came quite close but didn't appear to catch anything. I felt it rather strange to look across to other river bank, several hundred metres away, and know that, politically, it was another country.

Leaving Bangui we drove to the town of Bangassou from where we took a ferry across the Ubangui River, landing at a tiny place with the delightful name of Ndu. We had a lengthy delay at the ferry. Ahead of us was the Bedford truck of another Overland operator called Siafu. The driver had made the mistake, as he drove off the ferry at Ndu, of attempting to change gear when just the front two wheels were on dry land. The resultant shudder caused by the gear change, and the back weight of the truck had pushed the ferry away from the bank, meaning the Siafu truck was suspended between the river bank and the ferry. It took a bit of head-scratching and innovation before they managed to force the ferry closer to the shore allowing the Bedford to disembark safely. Fortunately, no damage was done. Keith made sure he did not make the same mistake when he drove off the ferry.

Zaïre was originally the Belgian Congo and is now known as the Democratic Republic of Congo. It is one of the largest countries in Africa and it was certainly a fascinating place. During the colonial days, the Belgians had developed an infrastructure of good roads criss-crossing the country but after independence in 1960, very little maintenance had been carried out and this was soon to become very obvious to us. We had to spend a night in Ndu and woke up to a thick fog, something I found rather surprising in tropical Africa. It took us most of the morning to clear customs and we had to send our cooking party back across the river to Bangassou to stock up with fresh supplies. We then drove to the small town of Monga to clear immigration and again we were delayed overnight. I noted in my diary that Monga: *'has a huge mission church on the outskirts, is a real frontier town ... some buildings appear to have been burnt out and there was some speculation as to whether they were the result of the Congo troubles ten years ago. It wasn't hard to imagine mercenaries ravaging a village of this type by fire and sword, rape and plunder!'* Just out of Monga we had to cross a small tributary of the Ubangui by a local ferry. This time the ferry was made up of three dugout canoes lashed together and large enough to take our Bedford. It had to be propelled across the river by man-power, making use of the river currents and back-eddies. There were several traditional dugout canoes on the river and I was bemused to see one propelled, at speed, by a Yamaha outboard. In the forest, not far from the river, we came upon a dugout still in the process of being adzed from a tree trunk. The lines of the pirogue, surrounded by a mass of wood chips, did not look exactly straight and the hull was still attached to the tree.

After crossing the Uele River by another interesting local ferry, the largest yet, we were into the African rainforest and the road deteriorated further; tarmac became non-existent and in lieu of proper culverts, tree trunks formed make-shift bridges over many of the little streams. This usually involved some tricky manoeuvring to get our vehicles across without mishap; potholes were huge and one morning we pulled out a truck, its Belgian driver saying he had been stuck overnight with one of his back-wheels in an almost bottomless hole! To make things even more hazardous, both sides of the road were lined with deep ditches, usually hidden by lush vegetation and our progress was not without incidents! Most of the towns we passed through had been built around a Catholic Mission and were very much as I had envisaged – dense tropical vegetation surrounded the small settlements, many of the European-style colonial houses now looking much the worse for wear; shops dark and cool inside, but with very little stock.

We stopped in the little town of Titule and that evening I walked with a couple of companions, to the chirruping of insects, the strobe-light winking of fireflies and the vivid flashes of wildfire lightning, to a local bar for a beer or two. We entered the bar and I looked around. A brick pillar in the centre of the building supported the wooden beams that held the thatched roof. I noted: "*The bar was a real jungle bar, banana-leafed roof, mud walls, lit by a Tilley lamp at the bar.*" On the wall were posters of President Mobutu Sese Seko and paintings, one of which grabbed my attention: "*One painting, askew on the wall near me depicted the raising of a flag in front of a grass hut in a forest glade. Marchers were approaching the flagpole and overhead two aircraft flew.*" It was the naivety of this painting by a local artist that "*made it so beautiful.*" Drinkers sat at tables improvised from wooden boxes sipping warm Makasi beer from the *Brasserie D'Isiro* while loud Zaïrean music pounded forth from a scratchy gramophone. Dancers rocked in time to the African beat. We were made to feel very welcome.

Early the next morning I walked, to the sound of the mission bells, down to the nearby Bima River. It was a lovely morning with mists wreathing around the palms and banana groves on the riverbank. Ghostly dugouts drifted silently over the placid river waters; it was an idyllic scene typical of the tropics. To a certain extent it reminded me of a passage in Joseph Conrad's 'Heart of Darkness', which was set in the Congo not so very far from here: '*Going up that river was like travelling back to the earliest beginnings of the world, when vegetation rioted on the earth and the big trees were kings. An empty stream, a great silence, an impenetrable forest.*

The air was warm, thick, heavy, sluggish.' I could see what Conrad was getting at.

That same day was the 8th Anniversary of the seizing of power by President Mobutu. The year before he had renamed himself Mobutu Sese Seko Nkuku Ngbendu Wa Za Banga ("The all-powerful warrior who, because of his endurance and inflexible will to win, goes from conquest to conquest, leaving fire in his wake") – a very grandiose title. In 1971 he had renamed the country Zaïre "the river that swallows all rivers." In Titule that morning, there were processions of veteran soldiers, police, militia and local female members of the MPR – Mouvement Populaire de la Révolution - marching proudly with a vigorous lateral swinging of the arms. In the middle of town a VIP rostrum had been erected and a corpulent, uniformed party official was taking the salute. He looked the epitome of a self-important, small-time official who has rather too much personal power, and plenty of available food!

A couple of days later we entered the town of Isiro, just on sunset, after *'falling foul with the local militia for not stopping as they were lowering the national flag. Some officious bastard of a soldier accompanied us to town and tried to make an issue of it but we acted dumb and apologised!'* Isiro is a largish town that is the capital of the Haut-Uele District of the Congo. The town had quite a large population of Greeks who owned many of the shops and '*seem to operate the black market.*' I bought a couple of small ivory rings here as in those days there was not the blanket ban on the ivory trade that there is now. Isiro also had a couple of good, Greek-run bakeries that made excellent cakes – something we had not seen much of since leaving Europe. We were delayed in Isiro a day longer that we had intended as a top spring-leaf had broken and two shackle pins in the back springs had sheared on our Bedford. We also had problems obtaining diesel as all the filling stations in town had run out. *'Luckily one of the local Greeks, named Phoebus, had some diesel'* which he was willing to sell to us, probably at an inflated price, but we were grateful to be able to proceed on our way.

Not far from Isiro is the beginning of the Ituri Forest, home to the Pygmies, or Mbuti as they are known in the Congo. We came across small groups of these diminutive but interesting people, the males being all but naked and carrying bows and arrows and the women looking *'like young girls although they had immense breasts.'* I traded a white shirt for a bow and several arrows. Other members of the group also traded various items. One of the Pygmy women *'very girl-like was overjoyed to receive two light scarves which she insisted on using as a brassiere, this was particularly funny as she only covered the top of her hanging breasts, leaving her nipples exposed.'* In several places we saw their basic shelters in the rainforests of Ituri, nothing more than a wooden framework covered with palm-fronds and leaves. We also came across a column of the notorious army ants crossing the road. Stories about the ferocity of these ants were legendary, so we just had to investigate.

Our vehicle had already driven over the column, so the ants were not in the best of humour. So braving the wrath of these angry myrmidons, we all managed to take photos, but there was a lot of squirming and yelping for about another fifteen minutes while rogue ants were removed from trouser legs.

We were now running parallel to the Ruwenzori Mountains, believed by many in the 19th century to be the fabled Mountains of the Moon of the Greek geographer Ptolemy. Mornings were particularly pleasant and on one of my early morning guard duties, I noted in my diary that I could see both the Big Dipper and the Southern Cross in the skies just before daybreak, a sure indication that we were getting close to the Equator. I also noted that the sunrise over the Ruwenzori foothills "*was particularly beautiful with the rays preceding the globe, like a Japanese flag.*" I also noted that even though we were getting closer to the Equator, the temperatures seemed to be dropping. A look at the map showed that we were close to 7,000 feet, or 2100 metres, in elevation.

We reached the Equator early one morning near the village of Musienene. There was just a simple wooden board with 'Equateur' painted in blue along with 'Mustari Wa Usawa' in smaller letters underneath, which presumably meant the same in Swahili. In red a traveller, no doubt Australian, had painted 'Blue was here' and there were some English names written in ballpoint pen. This high region of Zaïre was very fertile and in one market we purchased some very sweet pineapples, strawberries and, surprisingly, tree tomatoes (tamarillos) which I had only ever seen in New Zealand.

The spectacular Escarpement de Kabasha marked the western edge of the Great Rift Valley and we began our descent down into Virunga National Park at the southern end of Lake Edward, which had been named by Henry Morton Stanley in the 1880s. In 1973 the lake had been renamed *Idi Amin Dada*, a short-lived name which reverted to the original after Idi Amin's overthrow in 1979. As we wound down the escarpment we could see a number of individual heavy rain showers on the plains below, complete with forked lightning – a surreal effect. In Virunga National Park we came upon African game animals for the first time, including the African buffalo, various antelopes, hippopotami and elephants, confirmation that we had now reached the teeming East African plains. I had been rather surprised at how little wildlife we had so far seen in Africa. We had spotted a few gazelles on a couple of occasions in the Sahara, a few monkeys and baboons on rare occasions in Central Africa and just one snake, but that was about all.

Our last destination in Zaïre was the small town of Goma and the nearby active volcano of Nyiragongo which we intended to climb. I had always been fascinated by volcanoes and badly wanted to climb an active one. The closest I had been to the summit of an active volcano had been the Crater Lake on Mt Ruapehu in New Zealand, some years before. The lightly steaming sulphur-streaked waters of the Ruapehu crater did not seem to me at the time to be a true volcano. I knew this was going to be a different experience, as we could see the ethereal red glow in the sky at night very clearly from Goma.

We set off the next day with a group of porters, led by a Zaïrean army guide who carried a large spear and a banger for scaring elephants. The lower slopes of 3175 metres high Nyiragongo were thickly vegetated but we soon reached the steeper scoria and lava slopes where the vegetation thinned out. I was physically fit in those days and managed to keep up with the guide. It was dusk and very cold by the time we reached the hut where we were to spend the night. After stowing our gear, we set off in the dark for the crater, a further 30 minutes of uphill scrambling. A cold wind was blowing smoke and choking fumes directly at us. I was one of the first to reach the crater rim and caught glimpses of the fires of the lava lake far below, before it was obscured by the acrid smoke. As it turned out, only two of us actually saw the magma that night, which was disappointing considering the fiery display we could see from Goma the night before. We visited the crater again early the next morning, but the strong cold wind was still blowing directly towards us and the lava lake remained largely obscured. There were, however, magnificent views over the still sleeping town of Goma and further in the distance we could see the waters of Lake Kivu just starting to appear out of the pre-dawn gloom. The return down the mountain to Goma took around 3 hours, somewhat quicker than the ascent!

Our route from Goma took us across the border into the then delightful little country of Rwanda, one of the smallest in Africa. This was some 20 years before the horrendous acts of genocide that swept this little country in 1994. In 1973 it was hard to realise that the hatred between the Tutsi and the Hutu must, even then, have been simmering not far beneath the surface, but then we had little understanding of the underlying politics of tribal rivalries. From our observations the people of Rwanda were very friendly, far more so than those of Zaïre. After a swim in the warm waters of Lake Kivu we headed off into the hills on the road to Kigali, the capital of Rwanda. At the time Rwanda was likened to being 'the Switzerland of Africa'. This epithet seemed entirely appropriate as we set up our overnight camp in an area of lush hills, scattered with a patchwork of rich cultivated plots, banana and pawpaw groves, all overlooked by the brooding volcanoes of Nyiragongo and the higher Karisimbi on which we could see patches of snow. The inevitable crowd of young people gathered around our camp, all good-natured and a couple of members of our group, knowing that Siafu, the other Trans-African group was following us a day behind, tried teaching the local youth to say to this group, when they saw them: "*Piss off you silly buggers!*" Many laughs were had on both sides and, although the locals spoke no English at all, they seemed to know that the expression was not entirely complimentary. We never did know the outcome. The Siafu group did follow a day behind but then decided, against all wisdom, to enter Idi Amin's Uganda which was to have rather unpleasant consequences. We did meet them again in Kenya, but after their harrowing experiences in Uganda, it did not seem appropriate to speak of what was such a minor banality in Rwanda.

From Rwanda we crossed into Julius Nyerere's Tanzania. I wrote in my diary that to comply with Tanzanian immigration regulations then in force we had to adopt 'fancy-dress', which meant we could not wear tight trousers, flares, shorts, mini-skirts or body-fitting shirts, all of which were deemed to be indecent. As it turned out, little notice was taken of how we were dressed when we passed through Tanzanian immigration. This was a time of repression in Tanzania with the forced collectivisation of the rural population, although we were to see little direct evidence of this as we headed to Mwanza on Lake Victoria before continuing on to the famous Game Parks of Serengeti and Ngorongoro Crater. At a small place called Busisi we caught a ferry, the MV *Sabasaba,* for a 30-minute voyage across an arm of Lake Victoria to a point some 35 kilometres from Mwanza. I was on cooking detail that night and we spent time shopping for vegetables in the Mwanza market. I noted that most of the vendors, both in shops and in the market stalls, were Indian and that produce was plentiful and of a high standard, especially when compared to what had been available elsewhere in central Africa.

We entered Serengeti National Park by the Western Corridor from Lake Victoria and immediately began to see game animals, first zebras, hartebeest, wildebeest and numerous Thomson's gazelle. These were followed by giraffe, African buffalo, baboons, Grant's gazelles, a few diminutive dik-dik (one of the smallest antelopes) and the occasional hyaena. There was great excitement when we saw a large herd of elephants in the distance and this was followed by a pride of lions who also kept their distance. The next day we were luckier and were able to approach close to a group of several lionesses and their cubs. They were enjoying the sunshine under the shelter of one of the many rocky knolls scattered across the plains and took little notice of us. Later in the day, I was sitting on a vantage point on the top of our truck when Keith drove under some low acacia branches and one of the long white thorns became deeply embedded in the muscle of my upper left arm near the shoulder. A nurse on the tour tried to remove it, to no avail. Five days later in Nairobi I visited the hospital where a young Australian doctor '*dug around in my arm for about an hour before giving up. The wound was stitched with the thorn still there and I now have a very painful arm.*' The thorn never did reappear!

We stopped briefly at Olduvai Gorge where, in 1959 Dr Louis and Mary Leakey had uncovered a hominid fossil which Dr Louis named *Zinjanthropus boisei,* believing it to be a precursor of modern humans. The Leakeys were continuing their paleoanthropological excavations at Olduvai but unfortunately it was late in the day when we arrived and the centre had closed. We spent the night on the rim of Ngorongoro Crater.

There was a brilliant sunrise as we left the rim and drove down the tortuous road to the mist-enshrouded floor 2000 feet below into what is one of the largest inactive volcanic calderas in the world. I was impressed with Ngorongoro Crater and wrote in my diary at the time that it was like driving around a large zoo. Here we saw our first wild rhinos and came across a group of three male lions basking in the sun. These lions and the lionesses of the previous day were the only large cats that I saw in East Africa – disappointingly no leopards or cheetahs. The central lake in Ngorongoro crater was a mass of pink flamingos. We also saw African buffalo, eland, waterbuck, hippopotami, ostrich, both golden and silver-backed jackals and hyaena. I photographed a group of vultures and a hyaena squabbling over what had probably been a lion's kill.

We visited Lake Manyara National Park on our way to Arusha. This small Park is one of the most attractive in East Africa and is famous for lions which are often seen lounging in the acacia trees. We saw plenty of elephants, including one rather large decomposing carcass which we originally approached downwind, the stench of which was horrendous. We also saw impala, tiny dik-diks and many baboons and monkeys but, unfortunately, no lions.

Our last night in Tanzania was spent near Arusha within sight of Mt Kilimanjaro, the highest mountain in Africa. We could see the snowy peak clearly from our campsite and although we did see the first rays of the sun strike the peak, it was soon obscured in the morning heat haze. Later that day we crossed the border into Kenya and entered Nairobi by the Uhuru Highway and drove down Kenyatta Avenue to City Park campsite where Intertrek's first trans-African expedition officially ended on 16 December 1973.

The local ferry on the Uele River at Bondo in what was then Zaire, November 1973

The active volcano of Nyiragonga from the town of Goma, Zaire November 1973

Chapter 13 Hitching to Johannesburg

For the first few days in Nairobi I stayed out at the camp site, having my breakfasts at an interesting little lean-to shack known locally as 'Roastie-toastie' which served good bacon and eggs. I spent a couple of days wandering around Kenyatta Street in central Nairobi and on one day we took the Intertrek land-rover on an excursion to Mt Kenya which we accessed from Naro Moru. Mt Kenya is the second highest mountain in Africa and lies pretty well right on the Equator. Unfortunately, the weather on the day was not good, although we did glimpse Mt Kenya's craggy peaks through the clouds just before we left in the late afternoon. Except for several groups of colobus monkeys, we saw very little wildlife – just *'the grand total of two buffalo'*. I mentioned in my diary that: *'We must have been pretty high (I'd say around 11-12,000 feet) as I was affected by the altitude.'*

I had decided to stay in Nairobi until after Christmas Day and moved into the YMCA on Christmas Eve. This was, in fact, my first night in a room with a proper bed for over three months and, strangely, I didn't sleep too well. The YMCA put on an excellent Christmas dinner, of which I ate too much. On Boxing day I hitch-hiked to Mombasa with Noreen, a co-traveller from the Intertrek trip.

We had no trouble with lifts and were taken by a couple of Sikhs to their Gurdwara at Makindu, almost halfway to Mombasa. They stopped at a small cemetery to show us some graves of the victims of the 'Man-eaters of Tsavo'. These two maneless, man-eating male lions had played havoc among the labourers, African and Indian, who were constructing the so-called 'Lunatic' railway line from Mombasa on the coast to Uganda in the interior in the late 19th century. The lions were eventually killed by Colonel J.H. Patterson in 1898 and he later wrote a popular book about the lion-hunt called *The Man-eaters of Tsavo*. After a meal of curried lentils, potato and chapatti, we took leave of our Sikh friends and headed back to the highway where we soon picked up a ride all the way through Tsavo National Park to Mombasa.

After a few days relaxing on the tropical Indian Ocean beaches of Kanamai and Twiga near Mombasa where I saw in the New Year 1974, I set off south alone, hitch-hiking and catching local buses, back into Tanzania, to the port town of Tanga. It was here that the realisation that I was now on my own really struck home. I wrote in my diary that: "*It is one of the worst aspects of travel – to be deposited in a strange town and have to look for a place to stay.*" On first appearance Tanga appeared to be '*a squalid dirty town*'. After just a few minutes in the dimly-lit, rubbish-strewn streets, I found the cheap Tanga Africa Lodging House. That evening I stood in the street outside the lodging house, eating a mango and listening to the sounds of the town. There were very few motor vehicles about and I could hear locals chatting, loud radio music blaring from a nearby house and in the distance a muezzin was calling the faithful to prayer. It was a fine clear night, Orion was particularly bright in the heavens above and the mango I was eating was juicy and sweet.

The next morning, I caught a local bus from Tanga to a little place called Segera on the main Moshi – Dar es Salaam road. I found the African buses quite an experience, noting that they are 'usually packed to capacity with chatty excited Africans either going to or coming from, markets.' Hitching could be slow, as there were few cars around, but when I was picked up, people were always friendly. My ride to Dar es Salaam that day was with a group of four young Tanzanians and the journey was fraught with mechanical problems. During one of these stops in a village we visited the local bar, just a small room decorated with murals on the blue walls; on one was of a lion, on another a group of huts and inexplicably, between the bar and the backdoor, a mermaid! The barman lay stretched out asleep on the bar with the radio blaring. When we entered, two barmaids were summoned to serve us, the only customers, with lukewarm 'Snow Cap' lager. One of the men who had picked me up introduced himself as Hubert Temba, then a young journalist who has since become a well-known poet and songwriter in Tanzania. When they dropped me off at the Florida Hotel in Dar es Salaam, Hubert asked me if I would send him my impressions of South Africa when I got there, but unfortunately I don't think I ever did as I misplaced his address.

From Dar es Salaam I headed inland, hitch-hiking down the newly constructed Tanzam Highway. At the roadside just out of Dar, I teamed up with Sami, a Japanese lad who was heading in the same direction. The first day we got as far as the town of Morogoro where we spent the night in a building under construction. The next day we spent several hours fruitlessly trying to hitch a ride out of Morogoro and it wasn't until the early afternoon that we were eventually picked up by a large lorry transporting two large cast-iron collars to a copper mine at Ndola in Zambia. It was to be an interesting ride. Sami and I scrambled into the collar to find ledges and cross-struts which were ideal for us to sit on and watch the passing countryside and the game as we passed through the Mikumi National Park. At the unusual hilltop town of Iringa our Indian driver and his mate insisted that we saw the Yul Brynner Western 'Catlow' with them in the local cinema. That night Sami and I slept on the back of the lorry in one of the collars.

Next day the lorry developed some mechanical problem, but this was fixed at the town of Mbeya and after crossing into Zambia we drove overnight in pouring rain with Sami and I huddled in the back. It was a hell of a night. My sleeping bag was thoroughly saturated with rain-water, and water thrown up by the lorry's wheels which splashed through gaps in truck's flatbed. In the morning the heavy rain eased to heavy showers and I managed to partly dry my sleeping bag. I had bought this very lightweight sleeping bag in London, feeling it would be suitable for Africa. It was not much more than a space blanket (metallised polyethylene terephthalate [MPET]) in a nylon cover. This was then new space-age technology, developed by NASA in the 1960s and designed to prevent body heat loss. Through most of the trip it had been adequate, but this was the first time I found that it didn't keep out heavy rain – both from above and below!

Late that same afternoon we were dropped off at the small town of Kapiri M'Poshi when the driver turned off the main road to Lusaka to head to Ndola. A heavy shower of rain at dusk forced Sami and I to seek refuge in a small roadside building that was under construction. It gave us good shelter but first we had to appease the local watchman who, in a nervous high-pitched voice was screaming 'Get out! Get out!' when he first saw our shadowy figures, but his whole demeanour changed when he saw that we were non-African. He was, I noted: *'a funny little character who prattled on in a mixture of English and Swahili – it didn't matter to him whether we understood or not.'* He insisted we join him in a supper of 'mealie-meal', the staple maize flour of southern Africa, and dried fish cooked on a charcoal burner. It was quite tasty. We slept on the hard, concrete floor and in the morning Sami and I bid our funny friend farewell and hitch-hiked on to Lusaka.

Lusaka, capital of Zambia, was a big modern city and in the crush of the midday crowds I lost sight of Sami as we crossed busy Cairo Road. He just seemed to disappear and I never did see him again. I spent the night at the Lusaka camp ground before hitching south to Livingstone, receiving lifts from interesting ex-pat English residents who had emigrated to Zambia before independence when it was still Northern Rhodesia. That evening I walked along an illuminated path through the forest from the Livingstone camp ground to the mighty Victoria Falls on the Zambezi River. To say this was awe-inspired was an understatement. The thunderous plunge of the deluge creating wreaths of swirling spray, lit by spotlights gave the entire scene a mystical effect and what was most remarkable is that I was the only person there that night. I was also the only person staying at the Camp ground, sleeping in my sleeping bag under a baobab tree, braving the wandering hippos and elephants. I never saw the campsite sign warning of these dangers until the next morning! I walked back to the Falls the next morning, and down beneath the Falls Bridge which had been the rail link and crossing point between the two Rhodesias when both were British colonies.

I was now heading to Rhodesia on the other side of the river but to get there was not quite as simple as it seemed. Rhodesia (now Zimbabwe) was then under the UDI (Unilateral Declaration of Independence) of Ian Smith, who had consequently been ostracised by the most of the world's leaders. Rhodesia had had trade sanctions imposed on it by the international community and for all intents and purposes the country was isolated from its northern neighbours. To enter Rhodesia from Zambia I had to travel to a place called Kazungula, cross the Zambezi by a ferry, watched over by Zambian soldiers in a machine-gun nest, to Botswana, then double back to the Rhodesian border. I hitched a ride to Kazungula with some Africans who were travelling to Botswana. En route they stopped at a roadside stall to buy *'buckets (literally) of their local beer. It looks like dishwater...'* One of the locals here had a large bucket of caterpillars which he indicated that they would eat. He was rather surprised that I showed no revulsion, as I guess other European travellers had. They were not too dissimilar to the huhu grubs of New Zealand, although I had never eaten them either.

I crossed the Zambezi and after two short lifts, reached the Rhodesian border *'where the bastards wouldn't let me in.'* I was refused entry by Rhodesian immigration due to a shortage of ready funds and a telegram confirmation I had of my sea passage from Cape Town to New Zealand was not deemed sufficient. I had to return to the small town of Kasane which was then, literally, isolated from the rest of Botswana.

I was now in a bit of a dilemma. Kasane, although gateway to the Chobe National Park, was then just a small village isolated from the rest of Botswana except for the road through Rhodesia. There was a direct fair-weather 'track' south but this was impassable at the time. An American construction company was just beginning to construct an all-weather road through to the larger town of Maun. Kasane was situated on the banks of a tributary of the Zambezi and was opposite the eastern end of the Caprivi Strip, an area of South West Africa, now Namibia, in which South African forces were then fighting a guerrilla war. There was a bank in Kasane, but it was only open for a couple of hours when the banker flew in from Francistown – usually once a week. I was able to camp at the Chobe Safari Lodge and it was a Friday morning when I sent a telegram from the Lodge to my parents in Auckland - 'Send $100 Barclays Francistown Botswana' - and I was prepared for a long wait along with a number of other travellers refused entry for the same reason. One English guy had already been there around three weeks. Time dragged rather slowly and at one stage a couple of us thought we may be able to get labouring work with the road construction company but were given short shrift by the rather conservative American management. The river was pleasant, however, and I would spend some time sitting on the riverbank in the warm morning sun reading. On one occasion two otters suddenly broke the glassy stillness just in front of me. They were really the only wildlife I saw at Chobe, although I did get painfully stung by a hornet at the Lodge.

I was rather surprised when, on the following Tuesday, Frankie, the Lodge receptionist came running across to tell me my money was through and would be with the banker who was arriving from Francistown later that morning. This was a great relief and although I was delayed another day waiting to get a more acceptable confirmation from Sitmar Line about my voyage home, I was finally able to hitch to the border and try once again to enter Rhodesia. This time all went smoothly at Immigration and I was finally able to cross into Rhodesia, although an overzealous Customs officer decided that some books I was carrying might be inflammatory. One was John Okello's *Revolution in Zanzibar* and another was *Song of Ocol,* poems by the Ugandan poet Okot p'Bitek. I was told that if the books were passed by the Rhodesian censor, they would be sent on to me in New Zealand, but of course they never were. None of the books related to Rhodesia or South Africa, so really it was my first experience of decisions, even literary, being made on racial grounds.

    I hitched a ride on the back of a lorry to Victoria Falls. The driver also picked up a young African who '*was moving, literally, as he had a bed, pots and pans etc., to Victoria Falls to look for a job as a houseboy. He was so happy and excited, but I felt rather sorry for him as he will probably have a lot of shit flung at him in the future...*' Despite economic embargoes and sanctions imposed by African nations on Rhodesia there was considerable rail activity on the Falls River Bridge. A steam locomotive would shunt wagons, laden with coal, to the middle of the bridge which was the border with Zambia, unhook them and return to the Rhodesian side of the Zambezi. I was told that Wankie coal was essential for the operation of the copper industry in Ndola but due to sanctions, Zambia could not purchase the coal directly from Rhodesia. Evidently Zaïrean Government had no such qualms and would purchase the commodity from the

Rhodesians then resell it to the Zambians, no doubt at a profit.

I visited the Victoria Falls once again, now seeing them from the other side of the river. Viewing points here were further from the Falls but there were more of them. At the Falls Bridge I took a double-look at the white Rhodesian soldier on duty. He was clad only in briefs, wearing a slouch-hat and carrying his submachine gun slung casually over his shoulder, a complete contrast to the camouflaged fatigue-wearing Zambian soldiers in their machine-gun nest at the Kazungula ferry.

I hitched on down to Bulawayo where I spent a couple of days before heading back into Botswana. I had been warned that the immigration check between Rhodesia and South Africa at the Beitbridge crossing was very strict, but those between Botswana and South Africa at Mafeking were quite lax. From Bulawayo I hitched a ride with three white businessmen who were heading to Francistown and then with a group of Africans to a small town called Serule. After waiting at Serule for over an hour and not a single vehicle went by I decided to catch the overnight train to Gaborone, the capital of Botswana. The railway station here was quite delightful, and I wrote in my diary that it '*is just like a small European station with a large shade tree, small area of grass, a little fountain and rows and plots of flowers.*'

The train arrived in Gaborone at 6am. This city was named after Kgosi Gaborone, an important local chief who is said to have died in 1932 at the age of 112. The city is modern, and I spent the morning looking around the commercial centre before attempting, without success, to hitch a ride out of town. A train was leaving for Mafeking at 6 the following morning so I decided to purchase a ticket and spent the night by the railway station, sleeping in a culvert, which I had surreptitiously crept into after dark to escape the attentions of the local prostitutes who were hanging around the Station Hotel. It did rain a little during the night and my sleeping bag was a little damp when I scrambled out of my refuge to catch the train.

The train was on time and I was soon at the border station of Ramathlabama. Here I had my first real taste of apartheid, then practised in South Africa in the 1970s. I had been travelling 3rd class and at the border a South African policeman beckoned to me, the only white, to follow him. He led me past lines of waiting Africans to an office where the appropriate formalities were speedily completed. I was then curtly told that as I was now in South Africa, I would have to travel in 2nd class and was escorted to the appropriate carriage.

At Mafeking I left the train and was walking down the main street when I met Dafne, a Cypriot girl, who asked if she could hitch with me to Johannesburg. We soon had lifts, arriving in Zeerust on the back of a pickup truck. We had to walk through the town and were then picked up by what Dafne described as a *'typical thick Afrikaner'* who dropped us just a few miles out of town in the middle of nowhere, just as the weather was about to break. We waited for some time then just as it started to rain we were picked up by an Indian who took us to Groot Marico where we were picked up by an ex-pat Englishman who took us all the way to Johannesburg. Our new friend insisted that Dafne and I come to his home in Randburg for tea and sandwiches before he and his wife drove us to the Johannesburg Youth Hostel in the suburb of Townsview.

'Roastie-Toastie', near the camp ground in Nairobi served good bacon & eggs. December 1973

I hitched a ride, for over 1500kms through Tanzania into Zambia, on this lorry   January 1974

Chapter 14   Return to New Zealand

I spent my first few days in Johannesburg getting to know this large city, the centre of which I described in my diary as: *'a true concrete jungle.'* The skyline was dominated by the Hillbrow (JG Strijdom) and the Brixton, or Albert Hertzog, Towers, the former being the highest building in Africa and in 1974, was the highest in the Southern Hemisphere. They had been built for television transmission but there was still considerable opposition to TV broadcasts by some of the more conservative Afrikaans politicians.   Dr Albert Hertzog had been Minister of Post and Telegraphs when the tower, originally named after him, was built in the early 1960s. He once said that TV would come to South Africa "*over my dead body*," denouncing it as "*a miniature bioscope over which parents would have no control.*" He also argued that "*South Africa would have to import films showing race mixing; and advertising would make non-white Africans dissatisfied with their lot.*" The new medium was then regarded as the "*devil's own box, for disseminating communism and immorality*". It would still be another two years before television was introduced to South Africa but in the meantime, there was, from the Hillbrow Tower, a tremendous view over the city. In my second week in Johannesburg, after receiving the appropriate work permit, I managed to get a position with Kentucky Fried Chicken at their Joubert Park outlet as assistant manager and moved to the cheap 'Down Under' boarding hotel in Hillbrow.

My time at Kentucky Fried Chicken was an eye-opener. Working under the apartheid system with its vagaries and idiosyncrasies was interesting to say the least. I had come into the shop as assistant manager, the lowest position a white man could hold, while the Africans could not proceed further than that of cook. Most of our staff were Tswanas and none of them seemed to have the right papers to live and work in Johannesburg. They were arrested on a regular basis with Hannes, the Austrian shop manager, having to bail them out. I believe there was a 14 rand fine or 28 days imprisonment for not having the correct papers – way out of proportion to the so-called crime. One morning Hannes and I were standing by the shop door when one of our boys came racing up the street pursued by two Bantu policemen. He dashed into the doorway behind Hannes and the two policemen stopped. His black head then appeared over Hannes' shoulder and, with one finger erect, he happily told the policemen to 'fuck off!'. He knew he was now under the protection of Hannes and me, and as we were white men the two policemen could not touch him. It was quite a comical situation, but again, rather sad that things should be like this.

Local Africans would often come into the shop, buy a couple of pieces of chicken and ask sheepishly if they were allowed to eat at the table and chairs in the shop. They were always surprised when we said yes. For a time we employed an Afrikaans woman as a cashier at busy times during weekends. At KFC we had to reconcile the numbers of chicken pieces being used with the amount that was actually rung up on the till. We started noticing a discrepancy of several chickens unaccounted for. Suspicion immediately fell upon the Africans and Hannes told them that the difference would be deducted from their meagre pay. This caused an uproar with vehement protestations of innocence and a rather sullen atmosphere developed. Hannes, however, had noticed that when the Afrikaans cashier was on duty, the cash amount taken was always more than what had been rung up on the till, never under. This aroused his suspicions, so he ran a check one Saturday when this particular lady was working and found that there was already a discrepancy in the chickens used. Hannes said to me that no way could it be the Africans stealing the chicken pieces, so we ran a detailed check on the cashier. I wrote down what she asked for over a busy period of an hour or so on a Sunday, then Hannes came in and reconciled what I had written down with what the cashier had rung up on the till. When she asked me for a dinner box, which was three pieces of chicken at 99 cents, she had rung up a snack box which was two pieces at 69 cents. She would pocket most of the difference, taking care to leave a little extra in the till. While mistakes could be made, and it was not uncommon for the till to be slightly over or under at the end of the day, it was always well over when she was on duty and this is what had aroused our suspicions. The cashier was summarily sacked and the African staff were overjoyed when we told them what had happened. They intimated that if we had been white South Africans, that second check would never have been made, which to me seemed a very sad situation.

From that time on we had their complete trust and they had ours.

It was during my time in Johannesburg that the first token act, by the South African Government then led by John Vorster, towards supposedly dismantling apartheid was made. This was the removal of 'Whites Only' (*Net Blankes*) signs on the public benches and other seating in Joubert Park. These signs were something I could never quite get my head around, especially the separate footbridges over the railway line – one for whites, one for blacks. Did it really make any difference? Johannesburg at night was then relatively safe and I often walked from Joubert Park to my digs in Hillbrow at one or two in the morning after a late shift. I was never threatened or even felt threatened. I've since been told that I could never do that now. Occasionally I might see a drying pool of blood on the pavement when I walked to the shop in the early morning, but this was usually the result of inter-tribal rivalries in the early hours, often between Tswanas and Zulus who never really got on with each other.

I did enjoy my time with KFC but by mid-May 1974 it was time to move on. I was booked to leave Cape Town by the Italian ship the *Fairsky* on the 18th of June, but first I wanted to see a little more of South Africa, Rhodesia and Mozambique. So one afternoon, after receiving a Portuguese visa to visit Mozambique, I left Johannesburg by train for Pretoria from where, after a night at the YMCA Hostel, I began hitch-hiking up through the Transvaal towards the Rhodesian border.

The first day I made it to Pietersburg, now known as Polokwane, and the next day I reached Messina. Initially the hitching was quite good although there were some areas where rides were sparse. Once home I wrote a short account of this journey which now makes interesting reading:

'I kick a stone and watch the dust settle on my boots. I turn and look along the road, nothing is coming. I hitch my pack higher and carry on slowly. The afternoon is warm and sunny and it is pleasant walking in these hills. A small brightly coloured snake slithers away from me, disappearing among the roadside rocks and at some distance I see a troop of small monkeys in the scrub near the roadside. As I approach they move away and soon disappear into the trees on the hillside. I pause, and glance back along the road; a car is coming. I turn and face the approaching vehicle, my thumb out, but it doesn't stop. I am feeling quite warm and sweating slightly so I shed my pack and sit on a nearby boulder. The road is again deserted. I have been in the Soutpansberg for about three hours and it must be seven or eight miles to Messina. I think I must have walked at least half of those miles.

I have now been in the Northern Transvaal since the previous morning when I walked out of Pretoria. Since then my fortunes had been mixed. I had had no trouble in hitching a ride to Potgietersrus and after a short wait was soon taken to Pietersburg where I arrived in the early afternoon. As it was a Saturday the shops closed early, and it seemed as if the home-going shoppers had little room for a traveller. I spent all afternoon kicking my heels on the roadside outside of Pietersburg and ended up spending a cold night in the scrub. It was shortly before sunrise, when the cold got the better of me, that I began walking, mainly to get warm. An African picked me up shortly after sunrise and dropped me off in the middle of the veld. By now the day was hot and sunny without a cloud in the sky as I walked in these grassy plains, broken only by the occasional rocky kopjes, those distinctive knolls once the lairs of roaming lions. I had walked two or three miles before I was given a ride to Louis Trichardt, a quiet little town at the edge of the Soutpansberg. Here I had had just enough time to buy a bottle of fruit drink at a store before I was offered a lift into the hills and I had been walking ever since.

Several vehicles have gone past while I have been resting here, none have stopped and I feel it is about time I started walking again. Some three miles or so I reach the Verwoerd tunnels. The sun is getting low and as I wait at the tunnel entrance the shadows of the hills envelope me. It will soon be dark and I look around for a suitable place to sleep. I am just about to scramble into the bushes when I hear a car. I'll give it one more go. Thumb out, and this time it stops. It is a family returning home after a day's outing and I am taken to the town of Messina on the Rhodesian border where I thankfully book into a hotel.'

The one thing I still remember about the Soutpansberg was seeing a large graffito in white paint splashed on a steep escarpment - 'Legalise Pot.'

After a good breakfast I left the Limpopo Inn in Messina and soon had a lift to the South African border and after clearing immigration, walked across Beitbridge, over '*the great grey-green greasy Limpopo River all set about with fever trees*' to the Rhodesia side of the border. My primary school teacher, George Bell, used to often quote these words of Rudyard Kipling, so it was quite a thrill to actually cross the Limpopo, however, thankfully I did not come upon any '*bi-coloured python rock-snakes*'. There were some interesting baobab trees in the area, so perhaps these were Kipling's '*fever-trees*'. After clearing Rhodesian immigration, this time without any problems, and changing money in the town of Beitbridge, I began hitching and was soon picked up by an African lorry driver who dropped me in the bush in the middle of nowhere and it was late in the afternoon before I was given a lift to Bubye River where I noted that the river *'has no water in it, although I'm told that there is water under the sand.'*

My main objective during this visit to Rhodesia was to visit the Great Zimbabwe Ruins near Fort Victoria (now called Masvingo), and the next morning my luck was in as I got a ride the 210 kilometres to Fort Victoria, and after a couple more short rides arrived at my objective. This amazing complex of ancient ruins seemed out of place in the heart of Africa. When they were first seen by Portuguese traders some 400 years ago, they were thought to be the long-lost capital of the Queen of Sheba. Later speculation surmised they were of Egyptian or Phoenician origin or even the work of the legendary Christian king Prester John. Archaeological excavations in the earlier part of the 20th century finally proved that they were in fact of African origin. I spent two days exploring the ruins, scrambling first up to the Acropolis which stands on a hill overlooking the site and the next day spent time within the massive stone walls of the Great Enclosure. What was most remarkable was that I had the ruins to myself on both days, no one else was there. It did seem appropriate that when Rhodesia finally became independent in 1980, it became Zimbabwe.

I hitched on to Salisbury (now Harare) and quite by chance bumped into a New Zealander with whom I had worked in Sussex the previous year. Although he knew I was somewhere in Africa, I had no idea that he was, so it was quite a pleasant encounter. After a couple of days in Salisbury I caught the overnight train to Umtali (now Mutare) and after a short delay the train continued on to Beira in what was then the Portuguese colony of Mozambique. A vicious war of liberation was being waged between the Portuguese Armed forces and the Frelimo (*Frente de Libertação de Moçambique*) guerrillas. Less than a month before my visit the so-called Carnation Revolution had occurred in Portugal which led to negotiations being held that eventually led to Mozambique attaining Independence in 1975. At Umtali I noticed that I was the only passenger booked all the way through to Beira, which I thought seemed a little unusual. At the border, a little place called Machipanda, the diesel locomotive of the Rhodesian Railways was replaced by an ancient steam engine of the Portuguese colonial railways. An armed escort of mainly black soldiers with white officers of the Portuguese Army joined the train and I noticed that a couple of railway wagons, which appeared to be full of sand, were attached to the front of the locomotive. It was only later that I realised that this was to bear the brunt of the blast of any contact mine exploding on the railway tracks – now I knew why I was the only passenger going all the way through to Beira! Despite all this perceived drama, the journey was without incident and as we travelled further into Mozambique the train gradually filled up with Portuguese and Africans travelling to Beira which we reached just after dark. I checked into the grandly named Hotel Savoy for around $3.00 a night.

Beira is Mozambique's second largest town and a major port on the Indian Ocean. It had a Mediterranean feel about it even though it was full of young clean-cut Portuguese soldiers, many of whom gave me quizzical looks as I sat drinking a cold Manica beer at a pavement cafe. Tourists were not very common in Beira at this time but I felt quite comfortable here. I was intending to catch a bus south to the small town of Vilanculos, but as there had been a FRELIMO attack on a bus travelling in the area during which 12 people had been killed just two weeks earlier, all bus services were suspended, so I had to fly. The aircraft was a 10-seater of DETA airlines and there were, including me, only three passengers to Vilanculos and no other aircraft were leaving Beira at the same time. But when I reached Vilanculos my luggage was nowhere to be seen – it had been left behind! It was no good becoming upset as my rucksack could not now arrive until the next day at the earliest. Fortunately, it did, but only because some airline official vaguely remembered that someone who had flown to Vilanculos the previous day had reported a lost rucksack!

Vilanculos, now called Vilankulo, was then a rather pleasant seaside resort and gateway to the Bazaruto, or Paradise, Islands just off the coast. I had initially thought of visiting these islands for a break, but the Vilanculos area was very pleasant and the temporary loss of my pack was a factor in deciding to stay put. I set out on a long walk which took me past the local boat builders. Two wooden fishing boats were under construction and I spent some time watching the workmen shaping the keel with hand-adzes before walking on across the mudflats, scaring the many mud-crabs that were emerging with the receding tide. Just offshore a small overloaded dhow with a patchwork sail made its way slowly along the coast.

After two days, I intended to catch a bus to the town of Maxixe, then hitch-hike south to Lourenço Marques, the country's capital, now called Maputo, but found that the bus had been rescheduled for the next day. This delay proved to be rather fortuitous as when I returned to the Vilanculos hotel I met Graham, a South African zoologist and, Margie, his wife - and their pet monkey - who had just arrived. They had been searching and trying to film the elusive dugongs in the Bazaruto Islands. They were now on their way south to a place called Zavora and invited me to join them there. Unfortunately, they had no room in their vehicle, so I caught the bus to Maxixe, as intended, the following day. This turned out to be '*one hell of a trip*' taking us nine hours to drive the 240 kilometres. The roads were good but at every one of the frequent stops luggage, and goats and chickens, had to go up on the roof. Goats' pee dribbling from the roof was an extra hazard if you were by an open window. The bus was packed to capacity for most of the journey. Just before we reached Maxixe a back tyre blew but as the bus had dual wheels, the driver decided to limp into the town. I immediately set out hitching south and after one ride, just as it was getting dark, I slipped into the bush at the roadside to spend the night. Next morning, I was finally picked up by a lorry which dropped me off at the turn-off to Zavora. As the road was little more than a dirt track, I thought I was going to be here for a while but was picked up by the first vehicle that came along and soon met up with my new South African friends.

Praia da Zavora is a beautiful beach on the Indian Ocean, popular with holidaying South Africans. On my first afternoon here, I went with Graham in his dune buggy along the beach for a spot of fishing. On our way back we came upon a native whose hand had been ripped open by a moray eel while he was gathering crustaceans for bait. It had certainly made a nasty mess but the African seemed to take it stoically. We bundled him into the dune buggy and took him to a South African doctor who was holidaying at Zavora and he soon stitched up the injury. The small community here at the camping ground was like a microcosm of South African history; there was the Pretorius family, the Bothas and the Krugers with whom we had many a happy evening drinking and talking, with the sound of the sea forming a backdrop to the soft music from Graham's guitar. Zavora has a couple of large rock pools, protected from the open sea at low tide, with many varieties of coral, brightly coloured tropical fish and large spiny sea urchins; just ideal for casual snorkelling. I spent a happy week here at Praia da Zavora, fishing from Graham's boat for snoek (barracoota) which he sold to a local restaurant, sunbathing, swimming, snorkelling and relaxing with a beer at the *Font dos Pescadores*, the local pub. I noted in my diary: '*These have been some of the most enjoyable days I have spent for some time, but as all good things end, I have to drift on*' – after all I did have a boat to catch!

Graham dropped me off in the small town of Inharrime and I caught the Express bus to Lourenço Marques, now called Maputo, which we reached, after a delay due to radiator trouble, just after sunset. I spent just one night here then caught an afternoon bus to Mbabane, capital of Swaziland which I reached well after dark. Next morning, after a short walk around Mbabane which is situated in a rather pleasant valley, I hitched back into the Transvaal and was given a lift to Ermelo by a couple of guys who had been buying *dagga*, the local marijuana, in Swaziland. Ermelo was cold and the next day around Volksrust I noticed snow on the ground and at Ladysmith I could see the snowy Drakensberg in the distance. Just outside of Ladysmith I was picked by an Australian in '*a massive Chevrolet Impala*' who took me all the way to Durban.

I had to collect my voyage ticket from the Sitmar Line office in Durban and after a couple of days exploring the city I was back on the road. I made good progress out of Durban and with a number of short lifts had reached Kokstad that evening. I was on the road early the next morning and after a slow start I reached Mt Ayliff which was in the Transkei. There was little traffic on the road but my luck was in. After about an hour and a half I was picked up by a Belgian who was living in South African and was going all the way to Port Elizabeth and he needed company for the journey which suited me just fine. The countryside in the Transkei was rather beautiful and we stopped for lunch in Umtata, now Mthatha. The Transkei was not then the controversial first Bantustan, the so-called homeland for the Xhosa people. Two years later in 1976, it became the first of four ethnic territories to be declared independent of South Africa. Throughout their existence, they remained internationally unrecognised, diplomatically isolated quasi-states until their reintegration with South Africa in 1994. South Africa had been the only country that acknowledged Transkei, Venda, Bophuthatswana and Ciskei as legal entities.

The post-Yom Kippur oil crisis was now beginning to hit home and like many other countries in the world South Africa was experiencing high prices and dwindling oil supplies, so consequently fuel was being rationed. My Belgian friend had around four times the daily allowance which enabled us to travel through the Transkei and all the way to Port Elizabeth without any problem.

I spent a couple of days in Port Elizabeth and my most memorable recollection was visiting the Oceanarium and spending time by the dolphin pool – there was no one else around and I'm not sure if I was keeping the dolphins amused or vice versa! It was the first time I had been close to these interesting sea creatures and they seemed to delight in bringing me pieces of seaweed, which I had to throw back in the pool in an endless game of aquatic fetch. I was the only visitor in the complex and reluctantly, after a couple of hours, I had to leave these playful cetaceans.

It took me a further three days to hitch-hike to Cape Town. The first night I slept rough on the edge of the Tsitsikama Forest in an area known as Bluelillies Bush and in the morning I was picked up by an elderly Afrikaans couple who spoke hardly any English and who were going to a funeral in Knysna. They were pleasant enough but, of course, we didn't have much of a conversation; quite the contrast with my next ride from Knysna to George with a very talkative travelling salesman. The last day's journey to Cape Town saw a change in the weather. I was travelling with a young South African and as we drove over Du Toitskloof Pass we ran into snow flurries which, he told me, he had never seen here before. On the Cape Town side of the Pass in was raining heavily but even so I could see that the views were phenomenal. After being dropped off on the outskirts of Cape Town in the rain, I had problems getting a bus to the city centre. Local buses were passing but they were for 'blacks only' and so wouldn't pick me up – a sort of reverse apartheid. Eventually the rain got the better of me, I gave up trying to catch the right bus and I caught a taxi to the Youth Hostel at Camp Bay.

My last days in South Africa were spent exploring the Cape Town region. Besides spending time in the city, I took the Cable car up Table Mountain which is, of course, a must do and I travelled out to Cape Point and to the Cape of Good Hope. I really felt that I had reached the end of my African journey when I stood on the fabled 'Cape of Storms' gazing across the south Atlantic. From schooldays, the Cape of Good Hope and the exploits of early European navigators such as Bartolomeu Diaz who was the first to round the Cape, and Vasco da Gama who reached India, had fascinated me. The passage around the Cape was often turbulent and for many immigrants and convicts on the transport ships to Australia and New Zealand, the Cape of Good Hope was the last land they ever saw before disappearing without trace into the unforgiving maw of the Southern Ocean's Roaring 40s or Furious 50s.

On the 18 June 1974, I boarded the Italian ship *Fairsky* in Cape Town for the voyage back to New Zealand via the Australian ports of Fremantle, Adelaide, Melbourne and Sydney. This was my first visit to Australia, and although we didn't spend long in any port, it did give me a brief taste of the 'lucky country.' This voyage by the *Fairsky* was the ship's last run as an immigrant ship for the '£25 poms', and a miserable lot most of them were. Quite a few younger Australians and New Zealanders were returning home from South Africa and we were joined by some of the younger immigrants who welcomed the distraction of the more boisterous Antipodeans. 'Castle Corner', named for the South African beer of which a plentiful supply was taken shipboard in Cape Town, was established in a section of the ship's main bar which became the centre of the 'social' life for the younger passengers, much to the seeming disapproval of many of the older British emigrants. The voyage was fairly tedious – ten days at sea across the Indian Ocean – and the daily routine would end at three a.m. when the bar closed. Six-packs of beer would be bought; clocks were immediately advanced one hour, and two hours later, at six a.m., the ship began serving breakfast. The rest of the day was for sleeping, there was not much else to do. I remember one passenger saying how he thought it was absolutely scandalous that there was no pool, or snooker, table on board!

After leaving Perth, we did experience quite a storm in the Australian Bight, which caused some superficial damage to the ship and freaked out many of the passengers! After brief stops in the ports of Adelaide and Melbourne, we steamed into Sydney and under the Harbour Bridge to a glorious sunrise. This was my first visit to Sydney, so I spent most of the day exploring. Then, on a sunny afternoon, some three weeks after leaving Cape Town, the sand-dunes and headlands of Capes Reinga and Maria van Diemen appeared to starboard and I knew my first Overseas Experience was at an end. The first steps had been taken.

Charles & Jonas, cooks at Kentucky Fried Chicken in Joubert Park, Johannesburg. April 1974

Fishing boats under construction at Vilanculos, Mozambique
June 1974

Postscript

After three and a half years working at home in New Zealand for the Ministry of Agriculture & Fisheries, I set out once again and after first working and travelling in the USA, I returned to London, and soon had a position as a tour leader on the Asian Overland routes through to Kathmandu. This led to further adventures as a special-interest tour leader in places as diverse as the Thar Desert in Rajasthan, the Vale of Kashmir and the Monasteries of Ladakh, and the ancient Greek and Roman sites of Turkey, Jordan and Tunisia. These later travel experiences are related in my second book – **One Foot in Front of the Other – Full Stride.**